Filling in the Blanks

Standardized Testing and
the Black-White Achievement Gap

A volume in
Contemporary Perspectives in Race and Ethnic Relations

Series Editors
M. Christopher Brown II, *Alcorn State University*
T. Elon Dancy II, *University of Oklahoma*

Contemporary Perspectives in Race and Ethnic Relations

M. Christopher Brown II and T. Elon Dancy II, Series Editors

Filling in the Blanks:
Standardized Testing and
the Black-White Achievement Gap (2011)
by Keena Arbuthnot

Filling in the Blanks

Standardized Testing and
the Black-White Achievement Gap

by

Keena Arbuthnot
Louisiana State University

Information Age Publishing, Inc.
Charlotte, North Carolina • www.infoagepub.com

Library of Congress Cataloging-in-Publication Data

Arbuthnot, Keena.
Filling in the blanks : standardized testing and the black-white
achievement gap / by Keena Arbuthnot.
    p. cm. -- (Contemporary perspectives in race and ethnic relations)
Includes bibliographical references.
ISBN 978-1-61735-441-0 (pbk.) -- ISBN 978-1-61735-442-7 (hc) --
ISBN 978-1-61735-443-4 (e-book)
1. Educational tests and measurements--Social aspects--United States. 2.
Test bias--United States. 3. Educational equalization--United States. I.
Title.
LB3051.A7445 2011
371.260973--dc22

                                                    2011010600

Printed in the United States of America

Dedication

This book is dedicated to:
Southwest Dekalb High School's Class of 2003

CONTENTS

ACKNOWLEDGMENTS

I am grateful to all those who have supported and encouraged my writing this book. First, I would like to sincerely thank M. Christopher Brown for being a great friend, colleague and mentor. You recognized that I had something of importance to share, and you helped me to bring that vision alive. No words can express my gratitude. Next, I would like to thank the faculty, administration and staff in the College of Education at Louisiana State University. Special thanks go to Eugene Kennedy, Petra Hendry, Jas Sullivan and Zakiya Wilson; thank you all for your feedback and support. Additionally, I would like to personally thank Heather Durham; I am very grateful for your willingness to edit several versions of this book as your feedback was invaluable. I would be remiss if I didn't acknowledge those mentors and colleagues who have been my champions during my academic career. This includes William Trent, Stafford Hood, Sara Lawrence-Lightfoot, Katherine E. Ryan and Bridget Terry Long; thank you for all of your support and encouragement.

I would like to thank my forever friends. There are too many of you to name, but you know who you are. Thank you all for being in my corner. Additionally, I want to acknowledge my entire extended family. I am indebted to those that have come before me, and I am inspired by those who are coming behind me. Lastly, I want to especially thank Stephanie, Alfreda and William Arbuthnot; you are the best cheerleaders a girl could ever have. You provide me with so much love and encouragement. I hope I make you proud! This book is truly dedicated to the three of you, thanks for always being there for me.

INTRODUCTION

Nearly 10 years ago, I began a journey to understand Black students and their experiences with standardized tests. Ten years of examining a complex problem has produced some very interesting findings, to say the least. I cannot say that I have fulfilled my goal of completely understanding their experiences, but I believe that through my time in the classroom, my research and my work, I definitely know more than I did 10 years ago, and if anything, I am able to raise even more questions about this issue that need to be examined and addressed. It is my hope that as you read this book, you will not only understand the information, but appreciate the journey.

Filling In the Blanks is a book devoted to understanding standardized testing and the Black-White achievement gap. When we speak of the achievement gap, the common question that is addressed is, why do Black students perform significantly worse than their White counterparts? This book is dedicated to providing research and insight into this dilemma. It is my hope that you can appreciate the footsteps in my journey. More importantly, I encourage you to join in the cause, not only to help understand the achievement gap, but also to provide solutions on ways to close it.

•

ACT I

How it all Began...

When I graduated from college with a bachelor's degree, I had no idea what was ahead of me. Like most new graduates, I was just happy to have finished my degree, and I knew the world was my oyster. There was so much that lie ahead. As the summer came to a close, and I had moved to Georgia to find a job with a new degree in one hand and an ambitious spirit within, I had the optimistic view that I could conquer anything. Then the reality of life set in, and I was confronted with very few options. Although I had a degree in math, I was not getting the barrage of job offers as I had wanted. In my desperation, a friend told me about the teacher's fair being held at a nearby elementary school. I decided to go, despite the fact that I had no formal background in pedagogy, and I truly doubted that anyone would hire me. Surprisingly, when I walked into the crowded elementary school lunch room, immediately a middle-aged man dressed in a suit asked me what my degree was in. With all of the excitement I could muster, I proudly told him that I had a bachelor's of science degree in mathematics. I was anticipating a long wait in line along with the other applicants to inquire about the job openings, but he asked me to step out of line and to follow him. He took me into a nearby classroom and began to interview me for a position at his high school, a predominately African American school in the heart of Atlanta. I hadn't expected this turn of events; however, I went along with the interview. I shared my resume and spoke with confidence of my mathematical ability. In less than twenty minutes, he offered me a job at his school. This was just the beginning of the journey for me, the beginning of what would become my life's work and passion.

When I arrived on the first day of school, I was given a key, a textbook and directions to a classroom. What joy I felt to be teaching the next generation! I felt lucky to be assigned to teach both the advanced geometry and algebra classes. The year began as a whirlwind, and things were moving at light's speed. As a novice, I quickly had to learn how to teach, discipline, counsel, and fill out the mounds of paperwork necessary to function each day. By the second month of school, I finally had a handle on it all, realizing that teaching was actually the easy part. My excitement for mathematics was contagious to my students. Especially in my advanced classes, I worked with some of the most brilliant minds of our times. They were such an energetic group, always raising thoughtful questions and challenging not only each other, but me as well. They would push me to push them further. The excitement in the classroom and my pride over these children were enormous, and I enjoyed seeing the excitement in their eyes each day in class. In my mind, these students were the best and definitely the brightest I had encountered. The sky was the limit for each and every one of them. As I came to know them well over my 2 years of teaching, I felt their energy and was quite comfortable with their mathematical ability.

The turning point for me in my teaching was the day that we received their PSAT scores. I was so excited to see the scores that they would earn. I was confident that with their motivation and dedication, they scored in the top percentage of students. Instead, the scores were quite disappointing. The scores did not reflect what I had seen in the classroom. Not only did the scores underestimate their ability, but the psychological factors that ensued were even worse. As the weeks went on after receiving the test scores, I could see the disappointment in their eyes. They were not as motivated or as confident about their abilities as they were prior to receiving their scores. I began to wonder, what is wrong with these tests? Why are my students not performing at their level of ability? Are the tests biased against Black students? Additionally, has anyone recognized or researched the psychological aspects of taking these tests? As I contemplated these questions for weeks, watching the sad eyes of my students and seeing the difference in the classroom, I decided I would do something about it; I would forge forward to figure out what was going on. I would help.

I began to research the achievement gap, and quickly realized that I would have to leave the classroom to solve this problem. So I set out on the journey not only to learn about tests, but to fix them. I was determined to find out why my kids did not do as well as their White counterparts, and I was even more determined to solve the problem and to change the world. I wanted the sad eyes to go away.

That was over 10 years ago, and I am still on my quest to solve this problem and figure out the testing system so that I could answer the question, are standardized tests fair? Are they biased against particular students? Is there something that we are missing when we look to use standardized tests as a tool of success? As I have pondered these many questions over my 10 years in education and academia, I have gone in several different directions and have studied these questions from several perspectives. I would have to say that I have studied this from a both a practitioner standpoint and as an academic researcher, and hope, someday, to examine this problem from a policymaker's standpoint. Thus, this book is a compilation of what I have learned about standardized testing and the Black-White achievement gap. What is known? What have I learned personally? What more have we left to learn?

ACT II

And so the next chapter of my journey began to unfold. I had to figure out my angle. Where in the landscape of academia would I find the answers I was searching for? I knew that many scholars were studying the achievement gap and making these ideas known, but where was there an opening in their research? What had they missed? Where would I begin with this journey of understanding and hopefully providing solutions? As I researched schools and programs of study, I became intrigued by the area of educational measurement and psychometrics. And the more I delved into the literature on this field and conducted my research, I realized there were very few, if any, African American women in this field. I began to think that this may be the angle from which I could look into this problem. Of course it made sense that I was angry and frustrated with the tests! I wanted to learn about the tests to understand and give insight into my own questions. What was wrong with the tests? Why do Black students have such a hard time with the tests?

My questions brought me to the realization that I should address the test itself, not simply the *effects* of the test. It was analogous to understanding cars. Many people can talk about the different types of cars, drive cars, and some can even sell cars. However, to really understand a car and the way it functions, you must open up the hood and understand how it is constructed. You must learn all of its intricate workings, part by part, and then understand how these parts interact with each other. So when people have trouble with cars, they do not go to a car salesman to help them understand their problem; they go see a mechanic. This is the person who understands the way the car was constructed. After looking at a car long enough and using the tools that he or she has, a good mechanic can usually tell you what is wrong with your car, or at the very least, what is right with it. So yes, I decided I wanted to be a mechanic. I wanted to understand the *process* first and then look at the *product*. So I made my decision. I was going to get a PhD in psychometrics and educational measurement. It took 4 years to obtain my degree from University of Illinois Urbana-Champaign, during which time I met several incredible scholars and colleagues who challenged and inspired me in my work, all the while remembering the reason I came to school. I came to solve a problem. I took courses, wrote papers and designed projects, all of which centered around my question of understanding these tests.

My first semester in school I met a professor by the name of Roderick McDonald. He was a well-known psychometrician who had been in the field for several years. This older gentlemen challenged me in ways I could not have predicted. His course began teaching me about the way that tests were constructed. The course showed me the mechanics of test construction, answering questions such as: How are tests constructed? How are items written? How are they scored? How are issues of quality addressed? Dr. McDonald's course opened my eyes to the test construction process. I knew I had a lot to learn, but this was the beginning of my understanding, the course that affirmed my choice of studies. Halfway through the semester, we began to talk about methods of differential item functioning (DIF), and the light bulb went on. I learned that DIF was a method used to examine test differences at the item level. The basic process of the analysis was that if I looked at matched groups of test takers from two different groups (such as race and gender), this analysis could tell me which items favored one group over another. This is only one part of the puzzle. I wanted to learn which test items favored which groups. If I looked at the differences at the item level, it would unlock some of the reasons that such large differences are found at the test level. So off I went into the field of DIF to learn about differences in test performance at the item level. It intrigued me to have a tool that would allow me to see which items were causing the most discrepancy between Black and White test takers. Or in my car mechanic analogy, I was actually beginning to acquire the tools that I needed to understand the car, how it worked, and when it malfunctioned. Unfortunately, as I started down the path to understanding how to conduct DIF studies, I hit a bump in the road. I learned that many psychometricians and measurement specialists could actually identify these items that functioned differently for different groups; however, they could not explain *why* these differences occurred. I was shocked! I thought, "I have made it this far, and when I get to the end of the path there is still no explanation. That cannot be possible!" That would be like a mechanic saying, "There is a leak in your engine; however, I do not know exactly where it is so I can't fix it." I thought the whole purpose of being a psychometrician was to provide answers that explained problems with tests, like a mechanic finds what is wrong with a car, and then fixes the problem. I thought I could tell them where the problem was, and then fix it.

ACT III

As my time at the University of Illinois at Urbana Champaign came to a close, I had obtained a doctorate in educational psychology with an emphasis on educational measurement/psychometrics. I completed a dissertation that helped to answer some of the questions about the achievement gap from a psychometric perspective. My research examined the intersection between DIF and stereotype threat. The findings were quite interesting, and I felt they had pushed my research in a direction of understanding differences particularly in the testing environment. I then accepted a postdoctoral fellowship and lecturer of education appointment at Harvard University. This experience allowed me to meet even more scholars in the area of education who would challenge me and push me in directions that I would have never thought possible.

In this position I was allowed to construct a course that would be offered to master's and doctoral students in the Graduate School of Education. As I embarked on developing ideas and information that I would construct for the course, I began to take a glimpse at what I knew and what I wanted to know. I wanted the course to be both informative and challenging. As I put the course together, it was a culmination of information about testing, gender differences, racial differences and explanations of those differences. I thought this course would be a great opportunity for students to understand these issues. The only problem with it was what I would name the course.

After pondering this for several days, I decided upon the name "Test Fairness." I thought it was the essence of what I would present in the class. The name of my course received quite a bit of opposition, as some of my colleagues thought it was an inappropriate title. This baffled me! Why would Test Fairness be inappropriate? From my experience, everything that I was doing ultimately centered around the idea that tests should be fair. I changed the name to "Race, Gender and Testing," but the experience took me on a journey to understand fairness. This journey would uncover the differing views of what people deemed as "fair." In the back of my mind, I was reminded of the late 80s cult classic movie *The Legend of Billy Jean*, where Billy Jean King professed to the world that "fair is fair." And at the time, I had thought so, too. So I began searching for answers to what people described as "test fairness." I started by asking colleagues and mentors to describe their idea of test fairness. The responses were interesting because everyone had a different take on the issue of fairness. I began to do some research on fairness to enlighten myself and my students on how test fairness is defined, or better yet, how it is *not* defined.

ACT IV

Halfway through my tenure at Harvard I had the opportunity to work with Professor Ronald Ferguson. Dr. Ferguson had written two chapters in the *The Black-White Test Score Gap* and had focused his career on looking at the achievement gap. I truly admired Dr. Ferguson for the work he had done and the passion he had concerning closing the achievement gap. He saw the achievement gap from a different angle than I did. It was not only interesting but also enlightening to see other scholars working to address this issue from different perspectives. The next light bulb moment for me happened when Dr. Ferguson and I attended a lecture given by Dr. Roland Fryer, an economics professor and fellow at Harvard

University. Dr. Fryer's discussion was about his research that investigated the issue of *acting white* as an explanation of the achievement gap. His presentation and research were quite interesting, and I was intrigued by the direction in which he was going.

After the lecture I was invited to a small group dinner to discuss the presentation. In the room were several prominent professors from Harvard Law School, Harvard Graduate School of Education and the Kennedy School Government along with a host of students and fellow faculty. As the conversation began, I was intrigued by the multiple perceptions and ideas people had about the achievement gap. Each person brought in information from his or her own point of view. Some ideas were complementary, and some were divergent, going in completely different directions. The most profound part of the discussion was the realization that we all may have different views and ideas about these differences, why they occur, and what we can do.

As the individuals in the room reflected, there are several perspectives and experts that can be utilized in solving this problem. Ultimately, the way to answer the questions is to come together with solutions, not just *one* solution, but many solutions that will address the issues. This group of renowned scholars taught me a valuable lesson: I can work to solve this problem, but it will take more than me alone to do it. It will take a diverse group of people who may or may not agree on the issues but all share a common thread, which is wanting the best for all children. We all want them to achieve and be successful.

My last point is that we all have a place in this discussion, whether you are a renowned professor, a parent of a struggling student, a government official contemplating an educational policy decision, or a teacher teaching a group of kids. Each of us has a voice, and we all have ideas on ways to address this issue. We must decide to work together and make it a reality.

ORGANIZATION OF THE BOOK

The book begins with a brief description of the assessment development process and how the four stages of assessment development impact the way in which we understand and use tests. Next, a discussion concerning test fairness is presented. A historical background of the issues of test fairness is explored and a discussion of the current interpretations of fairness is included. The next section of the book highlights the test performance patterns of Black students compared to White students. Research has shown that in general White and Asian American students outperform Black and Hispanic American students on standardized tests. However, for the purposes of comparison, this book will focus specifically on differences between White and Black test takers. Consequently, this part will highlight the differences in test performance between Black and White students on K-12 assessments (i.e., NAEP), college entrance examinations (i.e., SAT, ACT), and graduate and professional school entrance tests (i.e., MCAT, LSAT, GRE). The magnitude of these differences on each of the tests and subtests is discussed. Next, the book will provide an overview of the varying explanations for the Black and White achievement gap. The explanations range from factors associated with the home environment, schools and teachers, economic and health related issues, as well as internal factors such as stereotype threat and acting white theory. This section provides an overview of the research that examines reasons that explain why Black and White students perform differently on standardized tests.

After exploring the test performance differences at the test level, the next chapter explores the differences between White and Black test takers at the item level. Specifically, findings from DIF research highlights the patterns of difference at the item level between matched groups of Black and White students. This chapter also provides a comprehensive examination of those items that have been shown to favor White test takers (i.e, geometry) in comparison to Black test takers, as well as, items that favor Black test takers (i.e., algebra) in comparison to White test takers. This part will conclude with a list of the possible explanations and reasons test items show DIF between Black and White test takers.

Part II of the book includes several research projects that address and show new developments in understanding Black students' standardized test taking experiences. Specifically, this part of the book will present the research I have been involved in, as well as, my insight and perceptions of the different test taking experiences of groups of students. This section is focused on introducing other reasons and explanations that can be raised to understand the different experiences of Black and White test takers. The first study in this section focuses on the test-wiseness patterns of Black students in relation to White students, specifically, examining how Black and White students approach the testing environment. The next study in this chapter examines the motivation and persistence patterns of Black in comparison to White test takers. Both studies provide a very interesting perspective on the test-wiseness patterns of Black students.

The next chapter highlights the research I conducted titled "The Effects of Stereotype Threat on Standardized Mathematics Test Performance and Cognitive Processing" that was published in the Fall 2009 edition of the Harvard Educational Review. This article includes two new studies that examine how Black students process test items in different testing environment (i.e., high- and low-stakes). The results from both studies provide a new and innovative explanation of how Black students experience the test-taking situation. The next chapter provides a theoretical interpretation explaining the causes of cognitive differences in test-taking between Black and White test takers. Together, the studies presented in Part II provide a new and unique perspective regarding the differences in the way Black and White students experience the testing environment. Part II will end with a chapter devoted to policymakers, academicians and teachers. This chapter provides recommendations for policymakers in reference to Black students and standardized tests. Next, the chapter addresses researchers and academicians and offers new directions in research and recommendations for ways to move the field in new directions. Last, the section provides practical solutions and strategies for teachers to use to help Black students succeed on standardized tests. The book concludes with a collection of letters written to several different stakeholders that provides a summary of ideas and addresses ways in which each group can approach the issue of the Black/White achievement gap.

AUDIENCE

The book will be especially informative and useful to several audiences. The first audience for this book will be academics who are interested in studying the Black and White achievement gap, specifically those who are involved in understanding patterns of difference and providing solutions to stakeholders concerning the differences in Black and White students' test taking patterns. The second audience is policymakers and government officials who are interested in learning about and understanding the experiences of different groups of students when making policy decisions based on testing. This book will serve as a resource to guide the policy decisions that are faced by our government since the onset of the No Child Left Behind Act. The third audience will be practitioners. Teachers are struggling to help their students achieve competitive scores on standardized tests, and this book provides practical solutions and resources that practitioners can use in the classroom to help Black students succeed on standardized tests.

PART I

TESTING AND MEASUREMENT CONCEPTS

As stated in the introduction, it has been quite a journey to be at this juncture in my career. Act I and 2 of the introduction showed how I discovered that studying test performance differences and the achievement gap was my passion and calling. Although I would have liked to have jumped immediately into conducting research to try to solve the problem, I first had to learn quite a bit about testing in general. This background information included learning about how tests were developed and learning about issues related to test fairness, and how people were able to make a determination of whether or not a test was fair. Lastly, but most importantly, this included examining what the achievement gaps looked like throughout the educational pipeline. Where were the largest gaps between Black and White students? Were there certain academic areas where the gaps were smaller? Did these gaps persist into college and graduate school? Additionally, it was important to learn about the research that had already been completed that provided explanations about test performance differences.

Learning the aforementioned information was instrumental in laying the foundation for me to gain a better understanding of testing and issues related to test score gaps, as well as setting the stage for further research in the area. Consequently, Part I of this book is devoted to providing a basic overview of these topics to provide the reader with background information about issues related to testing and the test score gap between Black and White test takers. The chapters in this part are strictly informative and are not an extensive or exhaustive reference on these areas. There are several books and articles dedicated to exploring these topics in much more detail. It is my opinion that the information provided will help the reader better understand the research and information provided in the remainder of the book.

CHAPTER 1

THE TEST
DEVELOPMENT PROCESS

"To understand what these tests do and do not measure, it is important first to understand how they are constructed."

—Claude Steele

INTRODUCTION

This chapter discusses the test development process. It is important to understand to some degree how tests are constructed in order to dialogue about the results or uses of tests. Therefore, it is natural that I begin this first chapter describing the test development process. In no way is this chapter meant to be an exhaustive investigation of the process; however, the material addressed in this section is an overview of the process. It provides a framework for later discussion about standardized tests and the Black-White achievement gap.

TEST DEVELOPMENT

The test development process is an iterative process that test developers employ to construct a standardized test. The Standards for Educational and Psychological Testing (1999) define testing development as follows:

Filling in the Blanks: Standardized Testing and the Black-White Achievement Gap, pp. 3–8

Test development is the process of producing a measure of some aspect of an individual's knowledge, skill, ability, interests, attitudes, or other characteristics by developing items and combining them to form a test, according to a specified purpose. (p. 37)

There are four stages in the assessment process, including design, development, administration and use. In each stage, test developers must make critical decisions that will guide the structure of the assessment. Willingham and Cole (1997) created the Figure 1.1 presented below to show how the four stages of the assessment process are related to one another.

As can be seen in Figure 1.1, each of the phases of the assessment process relate in some way to one another. The decisions made at each stage impact the decisions at all of the other stages.

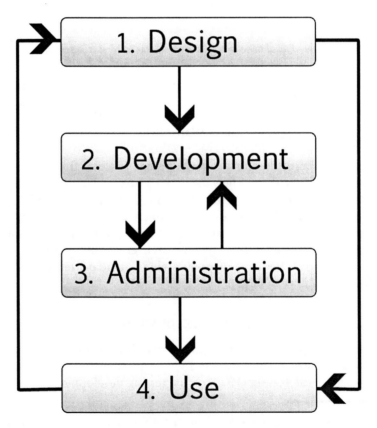

Figure 1.1. Four stages in the assessment process as pictured in Willingham and Cole (1997).

Test Design

The design phase is the first stage in the assessment process. At this stage, test developers attend to several issues. First, the test developer must state the purpose of the test. Stating the purpose is the heart of the assessment. It spearheads all other aspects of the process. It is important that the purpose is clear and well thought out, paying close attention to the other aspects of the assessment process. The second part of the design stage is developing the construct that the assessment is designed to measure. Vogt (1999) defines a construct as:

> a) something that exists theoretically but is not directly observable, b) a concept developed (constructed) for describing relations among phenomena or for other research purposes, c) a theoretical definition in which concepts are defined in terms of other concepts. For example, intelligence cannot be directly observed or measured; it is a construct. Researchers infer the existence of intelligence from behavior and use indexes (such as size of vocabulary or the ability to remember strings of numbers) to "construct" a measure of the construct, intelligence. (p. 53)

Likewise, the Educational Testing Service Standards (2002) defines it as follows:

> The complete set of knowledge, skills, abilities, or traits an assessment is intended to measure, such as knowledge of American history, reading comprehension, study skills, writing ability, logical reasoning, honesty, intelligence, and so forth. (p. 68)

For example, the construct for an algebra achievement test may be defined as follows: a test that assesses whether students have learned the concepts, processes and skills typically taught in first-year algebra.

The last part of the assessment design process is to create the test specifications. The test specifications provide the "recipe" for the assessment. The test specifications are a detailed list of the important aspects of the test. Specifically, the test specifications include the following information:

- Content and skills that will be measured by the test
- Test-taker population that the test was designed for
- How the results will be used
- Test format
- Timing of the test
- Directions

- Desired test and psychometric properties (i.e., level of difficulty, item discrimination, reliability)
- Item types that will be included on the tests
- Scoring methods
- Results as norm-referenced or criterion-referenced

The purpose statement, construct, and the test specifications provide the framework for the rest of the phases to follow.

Test Development

The second phase of the assessment development process is the development stage. Once the design phase is finished, the next step is to actually develop the instrument. In this stage, the test developer must develop test items that meet the requirements of the test design. The process of item development is critical in the assessment process. The developer must be thoughtful in deciding what items to include and the ways in which the items are written. McDonald (1999) suggests the following guidelines when writing test items: test items should be short, clear, definite, and simple. Additionally, when writing items, one should avoid negatives in the item stem and use simple, conventional vocabulary. The Standards for Educational and Psychological Testing (1999) states, "The test developer usually assembles an item pool that consists of a larger set of items than what is required by the test specifications" (p. 39) Once the items are developed and are assembled into the test using the information outlined in the test specifications, test developers are ready to administer the test.

Test Administration

The third phase of the assessment process is the administration stage. In this stage a test is actually administered to the test takers. The administration is guided by the information that has been outlined in the test specifications, such as timing and directions. The administration comes directly after item and test development. As can be seen in Figure 1.1, there is an arrow that goes from development to administration, and then an arrow that goes from administration back to development. Once a test is administered, it may return to the development phase. In particular, this may happen if there are reliability issues related to the test, or if the test and psychometrics properties outlined in the test specifications are not met. For example, the test specifications may indicate that the test should be a fairly easy examination; however, after analyzing the test data from a particular administration, it may be found that very few examinees were able to answer the questions correctly, or there were particular items that were extremely difficult to answer. The test developer may decide to modify the tests. This can be done in several ways, possibly by rewording questions to make them easier, or by deleting particular items that may be more problematic. There are a host of reasons why a test developer may decide to modify the test or particular items. Therefore, the administration and development stage is generally represented as a loop.

Test Use

The last phase in the assessment development process is the use stage. This stage is the process that delineates how the test should be used. What are the intended uses of the test? The use stage is not simply the last stage in the process, but it is actually considered in the design phase of the test development process. The use is of concern when the test developers are trying to state the purpose and construct, and even as they conceptualize the test specifications. Throughout the process, the test developer has to consider how a test is going to be used and what it will be used for. For example, the SAT and ACT were designed to be used for college admission. As seen in the Figure 1.1, the use of the test must be considered when the test developer is designing a test. There must be some critical thought concerning not only the intended uses of the test, but also the unintended uses, particularly how these separate issues will be addressed. Specifically, it has been argued that tests that are used for purposes other than those it was intended to be used for could be considered a threat to the validity of the interpretation of the test score.

CONCLUSION

Understanding the test development process is central to understanding testing in today's society. It is important to understand how tests are developed and, consequently, used. Although the process seems quite straightforward, it is often a fairly rigorous and iterative process to develop tests. As discussed in this chapter, the process is somewhat of a loop, with each component being central to the others. Therefore, if one component is deficient or substandard, the other components are affected as well.

In recent years there continues to be debate and controversy surrounding the use of standardized testing. Standardized testing is scrutinized by several different groups in and out of academia, including policymakers, the business community, parents, teachers, and students alike. This ongoing dialogue has been even more pronounced, given the recent increase in the use of standardized tests for high-stakes decisions. Often, these debates and critiques of standardized testing are focused on one aspect of the test development process. This is perfectly fine, as long as within the dialogue, the parties involved understand and conceptualize the other stages of the test development that affect the dynamics of standardized tests. For instance, many groups argue about the ways in which particular tests are used. As the arguments and debates about the use of particular standardized tests are discussed, it is critical that the discussion should include information about the intended purpose of the standardized tests. As discussed earlier in this chapter, that is always one of the most important driving forces of any test, what it was intended to measure. Those debating or discussing issues related to standardized tests should have a basic understanding of this process, showing that there is a need to focus not only on the *product*, but the *process* as well. The purpose of this chapter was simply to provide an introduction and a very basic conceptual model of the ways in which standardized tests are developed.

As issues related to testing are addressed in the remaining chapters of this book, it is important to remember the ways in which tests are developed. Understanding this process is centrally important when there is great public debate about standardized testing. In order to have a meaningful and thoughtful dialogue about standardized testing, all parties involved should have a basic understanding of the test development process. Understanding that the process of test development is not perfect, and that several decisions are made throughout the process that impact the quality of tests, will have meaningful effects on the ways we think about standardized tests. Additionally, understanding this process will help to disentangle issues related to test fairness and the validity of the interpretation of test scores and how these issues are related to the intended and unintended uses of standardized tests.

CHAPTER 2

VALIDITY AND TEST FAIRNESS

INTRODUCTION

This chapter examines issues related to test validity and fairness. When there is a discussion about differences in the test performance patterns between Black and White test takers, issues of fairness and the validity of test score interpretations are central to the discussion. Since test patterns show that Black students consistently score significantly lower than their White counterparts, many question whether standardized tests are fair to Black students. Additionally, the question arises, because of these large differences, are the interpretations of test scores valid? Essentially, is there some issue surrounding Black students or their culture that can explain why the tests could possibly be measuring something different for them in comparison to White students?

This chapter begins with a brief discussion of the definition and the various issues surrounding the validity of the interpretation of test scores. It highlights the potential threats to validity as well. The next section of this chapter addresses the history of fairness and how we have entered this point in the discussion. This will show the progression of these issues over the last century. Third, the chapter will discuss the current views and perceptions of test fairness and how test fairness is approached by test developers and members of the educational measurement community. It will also include a discussion about fairness and where the field is moving in reference to the differing interpretations of the issue. It concludes with information about where we should proceed in discussing issues of fairness.

VALIDITY

The foundational measurement concept of testing is validity. Validity is defined as an overall judgment of the extent to which the empirical evidence and theory support the adequacy and appropriateness of the interpretations from assessments for a specific use (Messick, 1989). The Standards for Educational and Psychological Testing (1999) states that validity is a unitary concept. It is the degree to which all the accumulated evidence supports the intended interpretation of test scores for the proposed purpose. The process of validation consists of collecting evidence that provides justification for the proposed score interpretation. There are several different sources of evidence based on test content, response processes, internal structure, and the relationship to other variables

Threats to Validity

Potential threats to validity basically show that a test measures either more or less than what it was intended to measure. These two types of threats are called *construct underrepresentation* and construct irrelevant variance. Construct underrepresentation occurs if a test does not measure certain aspects of a particular construct. For example, there is a mathematics achievement test that is intended to measure one's algebra achievement at the eighth grade level. However, the test does not include any test items that are intended to assess factoring. Since factoring is one of the major topics covered in eighth grade algebra, and there were no factoring problems on the examination, this could be a threat to the validity of the interpretation of the test score. Basically, a student's score on this test can not necessarily be interpreted as an accurate assessment of his or her algebra achievement because the test did not include items that assessed factoring.

On the other hand, *construct-irrelevant variance* refers to a construct defined so broadly that it includes consistent sources of extraneous variance associated with other constructs. Basically, a test is measuring characteristics, content, or skills that are not related to the construct being measured (Messick, 1989). For example, a mathematics achievement test designed for second grade students includes an abundance of word problems that require a significant amount of reading. This is an example of construct irrelevant variance because the test may be inadvertently assessing reading comprehension skills in addition to mathematics. A second example would be a test that is intended to measure college readiness is assessing test-wiseness skills in addition to the content that it was intended to measure. Since the test was not intended to measure test-wiseness skills, this can constitute issues related to construct irrelevant variance.

This issue of construct irrelevant variance is particularly interesting when we examine group differences in test performance. Consequently, if it is possible to identify sources of construct irrelevant variance that may have an effect on one group of test takers' scores in comparison to another, this information could be used to justify that there could be potential threats to the validity of the interpretation of the test scores. Additionally, some argue that test fairness can be considered a component of validity. Presented below is a discussion on the history and issues surrounding test fairness.

TEST FAIRNESS

As mentioned in the introduction, the definition of test fairness has been under quite a bit of scrutiny. It would seem rather appropriate that this section would begin with a well articulated definition of *test fairness*. Unfortunately, to date there is no agreed upon definition of test fairness, the Standards for Educational and Psychological Testing (1999) states that there is no single technical meaning for test fairness. What is known is that individuals have differing views of what test fairness means. One's view of test fairness is typically a reflection of an individual's personal values and judgment on what can be deemed as fair and how that can be measured. Nonetheless, in the last century issues of test fairness have come under scrutiny, and there have been several historical events that have contributed to our current understanding of differing ways people interpret test fairness.

History of Fairness

In the last century several events and developments related to test fairness have helped to shape our current understanding of fairness issues. These historical events are central to our understanding and continued dialogue of what it means for a test to be fair.

Cole and Zieky (2001) states:

> For about the first 60 years of the 20th century, measurement professionals did not, for the most part, focus on issues of fairness. During the late 1960s and early 1970s, there was an intense burst of interest in fairness research, but the results were less than satisfying. The late 1980s began the current era with its growing awareness of the complexity of the issues involved and a focus on fairness as an aspect of validity. (p. 369)

As stated by Cole and Zieky (2001) since the late 1980s there has been a growing awareness of the complexity of these issues related to fairness and validity. Presented below is a description of a select few events that have contributed to the current era of test fairness.

Army Alpha/Beta Tests

During World War I, Robert Yerkes, a psychologist studying mental testing, was given the opportunity to test 1.75 million army recruits (Carson, 1993; Spring, 1972). He developed two main tests, including the Army Alpha and the Army Beta tests. The Army Alpha test was a written test given to the recruits who could read. The tests were described as basic IQ tests that involved solving analogies, unscrambling sentences, filling in numbers, and other similar tasks. The second test, the Army Beta test was given to the recruits who could not read. This test included a pictorial test that included test items that used numbers, running a maze, and picture completion tasks. Yerkes claimed that the results of these tests demonstrated test-taker's innate intelligence. The findings showed differences between groups of European immigrants (such as Russian, Italian, Polish), and it showed considerable test performance differences between Black and White test takers.

Many researchers have argued how these tests were culturally biased. In fact, some scholars have uncovered how the results of these tests led to quite dire consequences for certain groups, in particular Blacks and Jews. Several years after the administration of the Army tests, scholars and researchers examined these tests and discovered that the Army tests were not measuring innate intelligence as initially stated. They were actually measuring American culture and environment. Nonetheless, the results from these tests had already had a significant impact on racial segregation policies, as well as immigration policies that restricted the number of certain groups of people, including those with low Army scores, from entering the country. The implementation and use of these tests were a gross example of the dialogue of whether tests were fair for particular groups. The consequences that ensued as a result of these tests highlighted the importance of the field to ensure that tests are fair to all groups of test takers.

Coleman Report

The Coleman Report that was based on the Equality of Educational Opportunity led by James S. Coleman was presented to the United States Congress and was published in 1966 (Cain & Watts, 1970; Coleman et al., 1966). This report was pivotal in helping to promote racial balance between schools. The findings showed that poor Black kids performed better in integrated middle-class schools in comparison to schools that were segregated. Coleman's work in this area had a large impact on educational policy. It was instrumental in creating educational policy that focused on desegregation. This report showed that issues of fairness in schooling could have an effect on Black student achievement, causing the government to place more emphasis on issues related to fairness.

Civil Right's and Women's Rights Movement

During the era of the Civil Rights and Women's Rights Movements, many began to focus on the inequalities in our nation. During this time the nation had become forced to be more conscious of what they interpreted as fair and just. This time period prompted academics in the measurement field to focus on issues of fairness (Cole & Zieky, 2001). During this period in history, many events had an influence on the ways in which the measurement community viewed issues of fairness, including the formation of the Association of Black Psychologists, court cases focusing on the use tests for employment, and the National Education Association calling for a moratorium on standardized tests. These events cause researchers to raise questions about whether or not standardized tests were fair to all test takers, or were they biased toward particular groups.

"How Much Can You Boost IQ and Scholastic Achievement"

During this same period, the article, "How Much Can You Boost IQ and Scholastic Achievement?" was written by Arthur Jensen (1969). The premise of the article was that there was a genetic component among the causes of differences in performance between White and Black test takers. According to Jensen, there was strong evidence that genetic factors were the reason why there were large differences in IQ scores between Blacks and Whites. This article sparked a surge of controversy. In the course of 8 years, this article was cited 638 times. This increased focus on test performance differences and the sources of these differences were addressed and studied by several researchers and academics during this period.

Golden Rule Settlement

The Golden Rule Settlement was a court case that was filed against Educational Testing Service and the Illinois Department of Insurance.

The case was filed by the Golden Insurance Company and five minority test takers who had failed the insurance licensing examination. The plaintiffs alleged that the licensing test for insurance agents was racially biased. The case was heard in and out of court several times (Bond, 1987). At the circuit court level, it was found that test makers could be held liable for racial discrimination, specifically if test makers knew that a particular test was shown to disadvantage minority test takers. This case was eventually settled out of court; however, the ramifications of the case led to an increased focus on fairness and equity in testing and the development of methods to identify item and test bias.

All of the above events have been instrumental in the way we conceptualize and understand issues related to test fairness. As can be seen, in the past century there have been several events that have explicitly or implicitly affected the way we think about and address issues of test fairness. The following section describes the current differing interpretations of fairness. As you read this section, I encourage you to assess your own perception of fairness. Challenge yourself to explore the other possibilities and interpretations.

Varying Views of Fairness

The Standards for Educational and Psychological Testing (1999) state that there are four different views of the meaning of fairness. Presented in Figure 2.1 are four possible scenarios. Each scenario depicts the four differing views of test fairness. Read each scenario and decide which scenario you feel is unfair or is an illustration of your thoughts on test fairness. Please note, all of the scenarios are hypothetical, and all references to certain states or companies are fictitious.

Category 1: Fairness as Lack of Bias

The first definition explains fairness as a lack of bias. This conceptualization of fairness rests solely in the test itself. Individuals who agree with this definition understand or believe that when one is speaking of test fairness, they are making the claim that a test is fair if it lacks bias. The Standards of Educational and Psychological Testing (1999) defines bias in two ways: item bias and predictive bias. These definitions of bias are related to differences at the item level and the relationship between test performance and other external factors. The person(s) who asserts this definition of fairness has the belief that if a test does not display item or predictive bias, then it is a fair test.

The concept is illustrated in Scenario 1. In this scenario, when asked about the fairness of the test, the president of test developer ABC speaks about item bias and predictive bias. From this perspective, he feels that if

Scenario 1	Scenario 2
The president of Test Developer Company ABC, when asked at a press conference about the fairness of the company's high school graduation test for the state of M, claims that the tests they develop are fair. Specifically, he states that each test is evaluated to eliminate or minimize item bias. Additionally, he states that the tests that have undergone studies that show a minimal amount of predictive bias. Hence, the president states that the tests are fair.	When the governor of State M was asked to discuss the fairness of his state's graduation test, he clearly stated that the graduation test that is administered to students was fair because all students in the state were given the same opportunity to accommodate them in the testing environment. Based on that information, he stated that the test was fair.

Scenario 3	Scenario 4
A test that assesses the degree to which police officers have the ability to be successful leaders is administered. The results show that the scores of Black test takers and the scores of White test takers on this test are significantly different. Specifically, the tests showed that the Black group of test takers' scores were considerably lower in comparison to the White test takers. Based on these differences in test scores, some have claimed that the test is unfair.	A teacher in State F looks over the math questions on the 8th grade state achievement tests and noticed that students were asked a battery of questions pertaining to geometry. The curriculum at her school did not require her to cover geometry with her 8th grade students. Because the students in her school had not been taught geometry in the 8th grade, the teacher makes the claim that the achievement test is not fair. Specifically, she justifies this because she states that her students did not have the opportunity to learn the material on the test.

Figure 2.1.   Four different scenarios of the meaning of fairness.

these criteria are examined and met, than a test can be seen as fair. Hence, fairness lies solely in the construction of the test from this perspective. Consequently, the importance of this perspective is that the responsibility rests on the test developer to ensure that the tests are fair based on item and predictive bias.

Category 2: Fairness as Equitable Treatment in the Testing Process

The second categorization of fairness is fairness interpreted as equitable treatment in the testing process. The Standards for Educational and Psychological Testing (1999) state, "Regardless of the purpose of testing, fairness requires that all examinees be given a comparable opportunity to demonstrate their standing on the constructs the test is intended to measure" (p. 74). it also states that other factors should be considered as well. First, one must ensure that all test takers are being tested given appropriate testing conditions. Next, all test takers have an equal opportunity to become familiarized with the test format. Last, group and individual test results should be accurately reported.

This concept of fairness is illustrated in Scenario 2. In this scenario, the governor of State M stated that the high school graduation test administered in his state was fair, based on the fact that all students had the same accommodations in the testing environment. This view of fairness is based on the notion that test takers be treated fairly in the testing process itself.

Category 3: Fairness as Equality in Outcomes in Testing

The third categorization is fairness as equality in outcomes in testing. This view of fairness is based on the assumption that in order for a test to be fair, the passing rates of particular groups are comparable. This view is based on the notion that if there are significant group differences in passing rates, the test is considered unfair. This concept is illustrated in Scenario 3 presented above. Since the scores show a significant difference between Black and White test takers, those who have this view of fairness would conclude that the test that was administered to police officers is unfair. This interpretation of test fairness has been highly scrutinized by the measurement and research community. Specifically, measurement specialists argue that differences in group performance alone does not indicate that a test is biased or unfair.

Category 4: Fairness as Opportunity to Learn

The fourth categorization is fairness as opportunity to learn. This view of fairness rests upon the idea that all test takers should have the same opportunity to learn or be instructed on the material that they will be tested on. The Standards for Educational and Psychological Testing (1999) state, "In many contexts, achievement tests are intended to assess what a test taker knows or can do as a result of formal instruction" (p. 76). This definition of fairness asserts that if a student has not been given the opportunity to learn the material, he or she should not be assessed on this information.

This categorization is illustrated in scenario 4 above, as the students in this scenario had not learned geometry in their class. Therefore, their scores were negatively impacted because they were never given the opportunity to learn the geometry material that was on the eighth grade achievement test. Because they hadn't had the opportunity to learn the material tested and their scores were being compared to students who had, the test was unfair.

The four varying views of test fairness presented above show how different perspectives of test fairness are conceived. More importantly, when we discuss whether a test is fair to particular students, we must justify the argument by explicitly stating the particular interpretation of what test fairness is and what it is not. This is of critical importance when individuals carry different views of what test fairness means.

Test Developers and Fairness

Test developers must attend to the issues related to fairness in the test development process. The question then arises, How do test developers address fairness in the assessment development process? The test development process, outlined in Chapter 1, has four stages. Test developers must address fairness issues at each stage of this process. This is done to ensure that the tests they develop are fair to all members of the testing population. Presented below is a brief description of the policies and procedures that Educational Testing Service (ETS) uses to address issues of fairness. This information is based on what is outlined in the ETS Standards for Quality and Fairness (2002). This will provide an illustration of the tactics and issues that test developers must attend to in order to ensure their tests and products are fair to the population of test takers. The standards related to test fairness were designed to do the following:

> help ensure that products and services will be designed, developed and administered in ways that treat people equally and fairly regardless of differences in personal characteristics such as race, ethnicity, gender or disability that are not relevant to the intended use of the product or service. (p. 17)

Consequently, the company states that their interpretation of the meaning of fairness is that construct-irrelevant personal characteristics of test-takers have no effect on individuals and groups test results or the interpretation of these results. In reference to fairness issues, ETS outlines eight standards. These standards provide detailed advice on the ways in which the company addresses these issues.

In reference to the items themselves, ETS outlines two major components to the fairness review. First, test items must undergo what is called a sensitivity review process. This review process includes careful analysis and evaluation of tests to ensure that they (a) reflect contributions of various groups of society in the United States, and (b) that test items do not include inflammatory language. For example, items that may be considered racist, sexist, offensive or negative toward a specific group should not be included on a test.

The second phase in reviewing the fairness of test items is to conduct differential item functioning (DIF) analysis. A DIF analysis identifies items that perform differently for matched groups of test takers. For instance, this analysis may find that when matched groups of male and female test takers take a reading comprehension test, certain items may favor one group over another. Consequently, when the DIF analysis reveals items that are found to show significantly large differences between matched groups of test takers, the items are reviewed and decisions are made as to whether the item will remain on the test.

The ETS standards are presented above as an illustration of the process that a test developer takes to identify items that may be biased toward one group over another. Similar practices are adhered to by other test developers. Although the methods to identify these items are well delineated and there are particular protocols and standards set forth regarding the way in which test developers identify problematic items, it is still unknown to what extent test developers adhere to these standards and how final decisions are made in terms of the inclusion or elimination of biased items. Ultimately, the process of conducting a fairness review is quite subjective.

CONCLUSION

I began this chapter discussing the definition of validity. It describes the two different threats to validity including construct underrepresentation and construct irrelevant variance. When we discuss issues related to test performance differences between Black and White test takers, of particular interest is construct irrelevant variance, or those characteristics, content or skills that are being measured that are not directly related to the construct that the test is supposed to measure. Consequently, researchers try to identify those characteristics, content, or skills that can be seen to cause these issues. Specifically, these are the ones that give one group an unfair advantage over another group. These findings have a direct effect on the validity of the interpretation of the test score. In the example presented earlier in the chapter, we discussed how mathematics word problems may be assessing reading comprehension skills in addition to mathematics which was the intended construct being measured. There could be other causes or sources of construct irrelevant variance that could be related to one's culture, environment or preferences. As we continue to understand and discuss the reasons why there are differences in test performance between Black and White test takers, we must ask ourselves, could some of the characteristics, content and skills we are addressing be regarded as a source of construct irrelevant variance? If so, how do these characteristics, content and skills affect the validity of the interpretation of the test scores.

Although there is no agreed upon definition for what test fairness means, it is important that there is a clear understanding of the differing views of this issue. As shown in this chapter, there have been several events over the last century that have addressed issues related to test fairness. These events have shaped the way we currently understand and interpret test fairness. In our current state, with the increased use of standardized tests for high-stakes decisions, it is important that we address and debate issues of test fairness. Standardized tests are now being used in education and in the private sector for a multitude of reasons, including grade promotion, high school graduation, inclusion in special education and gifted programs, college and graduate school admission, and for many job promotion and retention decisions. At no point in history have standardized tests been used so readily. Although standardized tests have been touted as the "Gold Standard," all stakeholders need to be aware and critical of whether tests are fair to all test takers. As previously mentioned, this can be a cumbersome task when there is no agreed upon definition of what test fairness is, making it quit difficult to prove or disprove whether or not a test is fair.

We must ask ourselves, what is the correct interpretation or view of test fairness? The answer is that no one view of test fairness is necessarily better than another. I contend that it is important to understand the differing views of fairness, as well as examine the issue of fairness from other vantage points. Consequently, when academics, policymakers, teachers, parents and students debate or discuss test fairness, it is important that one provides a definition of his/her interpretation as the basis for his/her argument. This approach will help to further the discussion of test fairness and provide a more balanced and worthwhile debate concerning the issue. As discussed in the introduction, when I was preparing to teach my course, some of my colleagues at Harvard and I had two distinct interpretations of what test fairness meant. In hindsight, it would have been a more fruitful and informative debate if we had initially discussed what our interpretation of test fairness was and dialogued about how those interpretations differ and why. No matter where you stand in terms of your interpretation of fairness, it is imperative that issues related to test fairness be examined and addressed by all stakeholders.

CHAPTER 3

TEST PERFORMANCE PATTERNS

INTRODUCTION

The purpose of this chapter is to provide a framework or baseline of understanding of the magnitude of the differences between Black and White test takers. Specifically, the chapter begins by highlighting the test performance patterns between Black and White students on K-12 assessments. Next, the chapter will highlight the patterns of difference on college entrance and graduate/professional school examinations. The information provided in the chapter will show how the patterns persist throughout the educational pipeline from elementary school to graduate school. Consequently, this chapter is designed to provide a basic understanding of the patterns of difference between Blacks and Whites. The tables presented in this chapter include the standardized mean difference, d, also referred to as effect size. The standardized mean difference provides a metric that can be used to illustrate the magnitude of the difference between two groups. The standardized mean difference or effect size is used because it provides a metric that can be compared across tests. Cohen (1988) states that if d is between .20-.49 indicates a small difference, when d is between .5-.79 that is considered a moderate difference, and when d is greater than .8 that is considered a large difference. Similarly, if d is zero that indicates there is no difference in test performance between the two groups studied.

Filling in the Blanks: Standardized Testing and the Black-White Achievement, pp. 21–32

The standardized mean was presented instead of the raw scores so that we could make comparisons across tests. Using the standardized mean makes it possible for us to see how large the differences are on the SAT, compared to the differences on the ACT, and so forth. It allows us to have a common measuring stick that can be used on any of the tests. For example, if you were on the market to buy a car, you may be concerned with the gas mileage of the vehicle you are buying. One dealership may tell you that one of their cars gets 30 miles to the gallon, and then you go to a different dealership and they tell you that one of their cars gets 45 kilometers to the gallon. If you wanted to compare the gas mileage of the two cars, you would have to put the cars gas mileage on the same metric. You may convert the kilometers to miles and then make a comparison. Consequently, when you made the conversion, the second car burns approximately 31 miles per gallon of gas. Since you have converted these to the same metric, we can compare gas mileage and we see that the two cars have nearly the same gas mileage. In the same spirit, the standardized mean difference allows us to compare scores across tests, so that we can gauge differences.

K-12 STANDARDIZED TESTS

To explore the test performance differences between Black and White test takers, from primary to secondary school, we must first identify a standardized test that we can use to examine these patterns. The test must include a national sample of students and be administered in both primary and secondary grades. Consequently, the best assessment to examine these patterns of difference is the NAEP assessment. It provides the most comprehensive picture of test patterns for the U.S. population.

NAEP

The NAEP is an assessment that is given to a nationally representative sample of American students (National Center for Educational Statistics, 2002, 2005). The NAEP covers the following subject areas: math, reading, science, writing, the arts, civics, economics, geography and U.S. history. The NAEP is conducted with students from the 4th, 8th and 12th grades. The assessment contains essentially the same test items from year to year. This allows comparisons from year to year to track student performance over time. The NAEP project is carried out by the National Center for Education Statistics in the United States Department of Education. Given that NAEP is a nationally representative sample it is used in this chapter to show the patterns of Black/White differences for K-12 students instead of other state administered or nationally administered examinations. Provided in the appendix is a detailed description of each of the NAEP tests.

What Are the Test Performances Differences Shown on the NAEP?

To examine the achievement gap between Black and White test takers, we begin with the overview of the differences in test performance on the NAEP. Specifically, Table 3.1 presented below shows the effect size of the differences between White and Black test takers on the NAEP assessments for each of the subject areas on the NAEP, as well as the content areas that are associated with each of the major subject areas. As can be seen, the composite scores of the examinations are in bold print and the subtests/content areas are italicized.

Table 3.1.   Differences in Test Performance Between Black and White Test Takers on the NAEP Assessment

Subject/Content Area	4th Grade	8th Grade	12th Grade
MATHEMATICS	**1.00**	**.97**	**1.04**
Number prop. and operations	0.93	0.94	0.95
Measurement	1.06	0.93	1.14
Geometry	0.90	0.92	1.08
Data analysis and probability	0.95	0.92	1.08
Algebra	0.86	0.86	0.89
READING	**0.83**	**0.85**	**0.71**
Reading for literacy experience	0.76	0.79	0.71
Reading for Information	0.86	0.76	0.71
Reading to perform a task	–	0.80	0.48
SCIENCE	**1.19**	**1.19**	**1.20**
Earth science	1.11	1.14	1.21
Physical science	1.15	1.20	1.19
Life science	1.08	1.08	1.06
U.S. HISTORY	**1.00**	**1.03**	**.95**
Democracy	0.85	0.86	0.80
Cultures	1.02	0.93	0.87
Technology	1.09	1.02	1.01
World	0.97	1.22	1.03

Table continues on next page

Table 3.1. Continued

Subject/Content Area	4th Grade	8th Grade	12th Grade
ECONOMICS			**0.96**
Market	–	–	0.92
National	–	–	0.97
International	–	–	0.88
GEOGRAPHY	**1.13**	**1.16**	**1.26**
Space and Place	1.10	1.21	1.32
Environment and Society	1.06	1.17	1.27
Spatial Dynamics	1.11	.98	1.07
WRITING	**0.62**	**0.68**	**0.69**
CIVICS	**0.87**	**0.89**	**0.84**

Table 3.1 provides details regarding the differences in test performance between Black and White test takers on the NAEP assessment. The standardized mean differences between Black and White test takers shows that on all of the tests, Whites outperform Black test takers. This is a well documented occurrence on most standardized tests. However, it is important to examine the patterns of difference between Blacks and Whites. What subject areas have the largest differences, and what areas seem to show smaller differences? Investigating these patterns of differences provide a clear image of the test score gap.

The findings show, on average, that we see fairly consistent gaps from 4th grade to 12th grade. For example, in the area of mathematics the findings show that at 4th grade the standardized mean difference is 1.00, in 8th grade it is 0.97, and at 12th grade it is 1.04. This shows that the differences in performance between Black and White students persists from 4th to 12th grades. This pattern is consistent for science, U.S. history, writing, and civics. However, the pattern is slightly different for reading comprehension, where we see a smaller test performance differences in 12th grade in comparison to 4th and 8th grade test takers. On the other hand, in geography we see the gap between Black and White test takers the largest at 12th grade in comparison to 4th and 8th grade test takers. In addition to these findings, the chart above gives details concerning the test performance patterns for all of the subtests on the NAEP assessment. These findings help you to see the magnitude of the differences and which specific areas there are greater differences (i.e., physical science) and those areas that show smaller differences (i.e., algebra). There are tables located in Appendix A-I that provide scaled score, standard deviation and standardized mean differences for each test and subtest presented in Table 3.1.

College and Graduate/Professional School Entrance Examinations

What Are the Test Performance Differences Between Black and White Test Takers on College Entrance and Professional Graduate?

This section covers the test pattern differences between Black and White test takers on college, graduate, and professional school entrance examinations, including the SAT, ACT, Medical College Admissions Test (MCAT), Graduate Management Admission Test (GMAT), Graduate Records Examination (GRE), and Law School Admissions Test (LSAT). The overarching goal of each of the college entrance and graduate or professional examinations is to help schools select students to enter their respective institutions. The scores on these examinations are taken into account along with other factors to help students gain admission into universities or colleges of their choosing. Although many argue that the test scores are not the only determining factor in gaining admission to colleges or professional schools, many are also aware that these standardized test scores are prioritized as one of the most important factors for entrance. Consequently, the stakes associated with these tests are high, and the results from taking these tests can mean the difference between getting into a particular school, or not going to college or graduate school at all (see Table 3.2). Table 3.3 provides a detailed description of the each of the admissions test outlined in Tables 3.1 and 3.2.

Table 3.2.   Differences in Test Performance Between Black and White Test Takers on College, Graduate, and Professional School Tests

Subject/Content Area	d
SAT	
Critical Reading	1.00
Mathematics	1.10
Writing	0.98
ACT	**1.00**
English	0.90
Mathematics	0.90

Table continues on next page

Table 3.2.   Continued

Subject/Content Area	d
ACT	**1.00**
Reading	0.90
Science	0.90
MCAT	
Physical Sciences	0.90
Biological Sciences	1.00
Verbal Reasoning	1.00
Writing Sample	
GMAT	**1.00**
Verbal	
Quantitative	
Analytical Writing	
GRE	
Verbal Reasoning	1.00
Quantitative Reasoning	1.30
Analytical Writing	1.50
LSAT	**1.20**

Table 3.3.   Detailed Description of the Each of the Admissions Test Outlined

Test	Subtests	Description
SAT	• Critical Reading • Mathematics • Writing	The SAT is one of the most widely used college admissions test in the United States. The SAT assesses critical thinking skills students need for academic success in college. The SAT consists of the following three subject areas including, Critical Reading, Mathematics, Writing. The Critical Reading sections include passage-based reading and sentence completion items. Next, the Mathematics test covers numbers and operations; algebra and functions; geometry and statistics; and probability and data analysis. These questions are posed as multiple choice items or student response (grid in). The Writing section includes multiple choice items that are centered on grammar, usage and word choice. Additionally, students are asked to construct an essay based on a prompt. Students receive a score of 200-800 on each of the sections of the SAT. The SAT lasts approximately 3½ hours and is administered six times a year in the United States.

Test	Subtests	Description
ACT	• English • Mathematics • Reading • Science • Writing	The ACT is described as a test that assesses high school students' general educational development and their ability to complete college coursework. The ACT is said to provide an indicator of "college readiness." The ACT is a multiple choice test that covers the following areas: English, Mathematics, Reading, Science, and Writing. The English test covers usage/mechanics and rhetorical skills. This portion of the test includes five passages which students must read and answer questions that pertain to their English skills. Next, the Mathematics test covers various facets of algebra, geometry and elementary trigonometry. The Reading Comprehension section consists of four passages and a set of questions pertaining to each of the passages. The Science Reasoning section includes seven passages that are related to science. Lastly, in the Writing section, students are given a prompt about a social issue and are instructed to construct an essay in response. The ACT lasts approximately 4 hours and is administered six times nationally. The subject scores range between 1 and 36.
MCAT	• Physical Sciences • Biological Sciences • Verbal Reasoning • Writing Sample	The Medical College Admission Test (MCAT) is a standardized test that is used for medical school admission. The test assesses the skills and knowledge needed to make students successful in medical school. The MCAT is a multiple choice test that covers the following areas: Physical Sciences, Biological Sciences, Verbal Reasoning, and Writing Sample. The Physical Science section assesses a test taker's problem-solving ability in general chemistry and physics. The Biological Sciences section of the test assesses a student's ability in biology and organic chemistry. The Verbal Reasoning section assesses students' ability to understand, evaluate, and apply information and arguments in prose style. On all of these sections, students are given seven passage-based problem sets to answer. Lastly, for the Writing Sample section, students are given a prompt and must complete two 30-minute essays. The MCAT lasts approximately 5½ and is administered nationally.

Test	Subtests	Description
GMAT	• Verbal Section • Quantitative Section • Analytical Writing	The Graduate Management Admission Test (GMAT) is a standardized test used for entrance into Business School. The GMAT is a multiple choice and writing test that covers the following areas: Verbal Section, Quantitative Section, and Analytical Writing. The Verbal Section measures a test taker's verbal ability with questions including reading comprehension, critical reasoning, and sentence correction. For this portion of the test, test takers are given 41 questions to answer in 75 minutes. Next, the Quantitative Reasoning portion of the test measures a test taker's quantitative ability with data sufficiency and problem-solving test items. For this section, test takers are given 37 questions and have 75 minutes to complete it. Lastly, the Analytical Writing section measures a test taker's ability to think analytically. In this section, test takers are given two writing tasks: analysis of an issue and analysis of an argument. Test takers are given 30 minutes to complete each task. The Quantitative and Verbal sections of the test are given as a computer-adaptive test at test centers throughout the United States. The test typically takes close to 4 hours to complete.

Table continues on next page

Table 3.3.   Continued

| GRE | • Verbal Reasoning
• Quantitative Reasoning
• Analytical Writing | The GRE is a standardized test used for entrance in graduate or professional schools. The GRE is a multiple choice and writing test that covers the following areas: Verbal Reasoning, Quantitative Reasoning, and Analytical Writing. The Verbal Reasoning measures a test taker's ability to analyze and evaluate written material, analyze relationships among different parts of sentences, and recognize relationships between words and concepts. For this portion of the test, test takers are given 30 questions to answer in 30 minutes. Next, the Quantitative Reasoning portion of the test measures a test taker's ability to understand basic mathematical concepts including arithmetic, algebra, geometry and data analysis, quantitative reasoning, and problem-solving in a quantitative setting. For this section, test takers are given 28 questions and have 45 minutes to complete it. Lastly, the Analytical Writing section measures a test taker's ability think analytically and clearly express their logic and reasoning. For this section, test takers are given two writing tasks. They are given 45 minutes to complete one task and are given 30 minutes to complete the other. The GRE is a computer-based test that is administered at test centers throughout the United States. The test typically takes close to 4 hours to complete. The score in each of the subtests ranges between 200 and 800 points. |
| LSAT | • Reading Comprehension
• Analytical Reasoning
• Logical Reasoning | The Law School Admission Test (LSAT) is a standardized test used for entrance into law schools. The test is designed to measure the skills necessary for admission to law school. The LSAT is a multiple choice and writing test that includes the following question types: Reading Comprehension, Analytical Reasoning, and Logical Reasoning. The verbal section measures a test taker's verbal ability with questions including reading comprehension, critical reasoning, and sentence correction. Each section of the tests lasts 35 minutes, and there are two logical reasoning sections. Additionally, there is a 35 minute writing sample that is administered as well. The LSAT is administered four times a year at test centers throughout the United States and across the world. The test typically takes nearly half a day to complete. The scores on the LSAT range from 120 to 180. |

Tables 3.4-3.11 present the test performance patterns of White and Black students on college, graduate, and professional or graduate school entrance tests. The tables shows the effect size of the differences for Black and White students on each of the tests. It is important to note that these tests differ from the NAEP assessment results because the participants on these examinations elected to take these exams, and likewise, had a choice over which exam they would take. For instance, only those students who are interested in going to law school would choose to take the LSAT examination. Therefore, the patterns that are presented in this section are based on a selected sample, not a representative sample like NAEP examinations.

Tables 3.4-3.11 show the test score patterns of difference between White and Black test takers on college, graduate, and professional school entrance examinations. Overall we see that on most college, graduate, and professional school entrance tests, the standard mean difference in test performance is approximately one. As previously mentioned in this chapter, that is a larger difference in test performance. We see even large differences in performance on the GRE, with differences that reach as high as 1.50. In addition to examining the differences at the test level, the standardized mean differences are shown for each of the subtest as well, with the exception for the LSAT.

Table 3.4.   Average Scores and Effect Sizes[*] for the 2009 SAT[**]

	Critical Reading		*Math*		*Writing*	
	Average	*d*	*Average*	*d*	*Average*	*d*
African American/Black	429	1.0	426	1.1	421	.98
White/Caucasian American	528		536		517	

Note: Effect size is calculated using the following standard deviation for African American/Blacks (Critical Reading: 96; Mathematics: 97; Writing: 93) White/Caucasian (Critical Reading: 102; Mathematics: 103; Writing: 102)

Table 3.5.   Average Scores and Effect Sizes[*] for the 2005 ACT[**]

	Composite		*English*		*Mathematics*	
	Average	*d*	*Average*	*d*	*Average*	*d*
African American/Black	17.0	1.0	16.2	0.9	16.8	0.9
White/Caucasian American	21.9	–	21.5	–	21.5	–

Note: Effect sizes were calculated by dividing the difference between the groups by the overall standard deviation (Composite: 4.9; English: 5.9; Mathematics: 5.0; Reading: 6.0; and Science: 4.6).

Table 3.6.   Average Scores and Effect Sizes[*] for the 2005 ACT[**]

	Reading		*Science*	
	Average	*d*	*Average*	*d*
African American/Black	17.0	0.9	17.0	0.9
White/Caucasian American	22.3	–	22.3	–

Note: Effect sizes were calculated by dividing the difference between the groups by the overall standard deviation (Composite: 4.9; English: 5.9; Mathematics: 5.0; Reading: 6.0; and Science: 4.6).

Table 3.7.   Average Scores and Effect Sizes[*] for the 2000 MCAT[**]

	Verbal Reasoning		Physical Sciences		Biological Sciences	
	Average	d	Average	d	Average	d
African American/ Black	6.0	1.0	6.3	0.9	6.3	1.0
White	8.3	–	8.4	–	8.6	–

* Effect sizes were calculated by dividing the difference between the focal group (minority groups) and the reference group (Whites) by the overall standard deviation (2.4).

Table 3.8.   Average Scores and Effect Sizes* for the 2004-2005 GMAT**

	Total Score	
	Average	d
African American/Black	425	−1.1
White	532	–

* Effect sizes were calculated by dividing the difference between the groups Scaled Score by the **estimated** overall standard deviation (100).

Table 3.9.   Average Scores and Effect Sizes[*] for the 1999-2000 GRE[**]

	Verbal		Quantitative		Analytical	
	Average	d	Average	d	Average	d
African American/ Black	392	1.0	419	1.3	427	1.5
White	490	–	547	–	572	–

* Effect sizes were calculated by dividing the difference between the groups Scaled Score by the **estimated** overall standard deviation (100). The analytical score in this table is based on the analytical section given during this time period. The analytical section was slightly different and was not a giving as a writing prompt.

Table 3.10.   Average Scores and Effect Sizes* for the 2003-2004 LSAT**

	Total Score		
	Average	SD	d
African American/Black	142.43	8.48	1.2
White	152.47	8.71	–

Table 3.11. Effect Sizes of Differences on College and Graduate/Professional School Entrance Examinations

Subject/Content Area	D
SAT	
Critical Reading	1.00
Mathematics	1.10
Writing	0.98
ACT	**1.0**
English	0.90
Mathematics	0.90
Reading	0.90
Science	0.90
MCAT	
Physical Sciences	0.90
Biological Sciences	1.00
Verbal Reasoning	1.00
Writing Sample	
GMAT	**1.00**
Verbal	
Quantitative	
Analytical Writing	
GRE	
Verbal Reasoning	1.00
Quantitative Reasoning	1.30
Analytical Writing	1.50
LSAT	**1.20**

What Are the Numbers Telling Us?

The findings for the college and graduate/professional school examination are somewhat consistent to what we find at the K-12 level. What does this mean? How do these numbers equate to the bigger picture. How does this help us understand the test score gap? We can see from the tables presented in this chapter that yes, Black students are consistently underperforming White students in all academic areas. Additionally, these differences persist throughout college and graduate school years. More specifically, these differences are large. As presented in the chapter, a standardized mean difference greater than .7 is considered a large difference in performance. As can be seen, we see large differences on mostly all of the tests and subtests. Ultimately, what does this mean? It means we have a grave problem that we as a society must address, given the fact that all students, regardless of color, are guaranteed a public education. It is not only our right, but our duty to find out if why particular groups are scoring significantly differently on the tests. The question is, are these differences real differences in achievement, or is there something about the test or one's environment that affects test performance? Getting to the bottom of our educational crisis is most important.

As many have coined, it is the most important dilemma our nation is facing. Is our educational system failing our students, or is it benefiting one group of students over another? What is the answer? These questions are not only important to academicians, they should be important to all citizens of the United States. We should be committed to ensuring equitable educational opportunities for all students. So, the story behind the numbers is that we have two distinctly different groups of test takers. The differences are so large that we have to conclude that these populations of test takers are significantly different in some way. What are the contributing factors to this dilemma? What is different for White test takers in comparison to Black test takers? There are some quite obvious differences we can derive based on the plight of the Black community in terms of its racialized history and the opportunities that were not afforded to those of Black ancestry; however, in our society today, what could be the reason or explanation that could cause our groups to perform so differently, and what is this saying about us as a society? Many have pondered these questions and have devoted enormous time and effort to unravel the intricacies of these differences to help explain the achievement gap.

This chapter was intended to create a mental picture for the reader, a picture of the dilemma we are facing. The picture that was created in this chapter was intended to solidify and justify why it is of the utmost of importance to continue conducting research in this area. Researchers for decades have been grappling with the issues surrounding the Black/ White achievement gap. Consequently, the following chapter outlines some of the explanations that have been raised to explain the sources of these differences.

CHAPTER 4

SOURCES OF THE BLACK-WHITE WHITE ACHIEVEMENT GAP

INTRODUCTION

The previous chapters have highlighted the achievement gap patterns between White and Black test takers on standardized tests. On average, the gap was approximately one standard deviation on most assessments, including both K-12 and college entrance and graduate or professional school entrance examinations. The patterns of difference have created a large amount of interest in what the reasons are for these marked differences. Why are we seeing consistent patterns of differences between Black and White test takers? The answer to this question is not simple. There are several pieces to this puzzle we must put together in order to clearly understand these differences. First, many want to know why the gaps exist and whether there are ways that would allow us to remedy the causes of these gaps in an effort to reduce or eliminate the achievement gap. There has been extensive research that has examined the causes and reasons for these differences from several different perspectives. Consequently, the purpose of this chapter is to present a brief overview of the variety of explanations and theories that have been hypothesized to explain and understand the achievement gap between White and Black test takers.

Filling in the Blanks: Standardized Testing and the Black-White Achievement Gap, pp. 33–45

This chapter is not designed to provide a comprehensive report of the differing views; however, it is a snapshot of the explanations that have been shown to help understand the differences. The chapter will end with a detailed examination and discussion of the explanations that are directly related to the student in the testing environment. This is central to the purpose and information provided in the remainder of this book.

SOURCES OF THE BLACK-WHITE ACHIEVEMENT GAP

Several research studies have investigated the different sources that could explain test score differences between Black and White test takers. As Claude Steele stated in his expert testimony given in the case *Gratz v. Bollinger* (2003):

> many factors including heredity may underlie scholastic aptitude, but even the highest estimates of hereditary influence allow for substantial influence of experiential factors. This means that one's performance on these tests can be influenced by one's experience, by one's cultural background, by one's access to schooling and cultural perspectives, attitudes, and know-hows that might favor test performance, by the extent to which one's peers value school achievement, by the nature of one's dinner table conversation, and so on.

This chapter examines the various explanations of test performance differences. It begins by focusing on explanations based on the following categories: (a) school- related factors, (b) factors related to teachers, (c) family factors, and (d) factors related to the local community. Each of the sections provide a brief overview of research findings that show how these factors may contribute to the achievement gap between Black and White students. The chapter ends with descriptions of sources and factors that contribute to the Black and White achievement gap that are directly related to the student and the test environment including the following: (a) acting White, (b) stereotype threat, (c) test anxiety, motivation and self-efficacy, (d) test-wiseness, and (e) cognitive processing. Table 4.1 provides an overview of the factors that could contribute to the achievement gap between Black and White test takers.

School Factors

To begin discussing the factors that have been raised to explain the test performance differences between Black and White test takers, it seems logical to begin with those factors that are directly related to a student's school. Presented below are the school-related factors that some researchers have derived that have an impact on differential performance between Black and White test takers.

Table 4.1.   Factors That Contribute to Achievement Gaps

School Factors	*Factors in the Local Community*
Student Expenditures and Funding	Economic opportunity
Tracking	Access to health and social services
Academic Rigor	Community safety
Instructional Leadership	Access to child care and after school
School Safety	programs
	Access to libraries, museums, etc.

Teacher Centered Factors	*Family Factors*
Teacher certification	Socioeconomic Status
Experience of teachers	Heredity
Expectations of students	Home Environment
Access to educational support materials	Diet and nutrition
Cultural sensitivity	Mobility
	Primary language spoken at home

Student Centered Factors		
Acting White	Stereotype Threat	Test Anxiety
Motivation	Self-Efficacy	Test-Wisenes
Cognitive Processing		

Per Student Expenditures

Factors related to school funding have been raised as a primary source or explanation for why there are large differences in test performance between Black and White test takers. Research has shown that on average, Black students tend to go high poverty, high minority schools. Consequently, those schools that have high poverty, high minority students tend to have significantly less funding per pupil in comparison to schools that majority students attend. For instance, in the state of Illinois, the New Trier Township high school district which, has a racial composition of 87.9% White and 0.6% Black spends $19,720 per pupil, while the Harvey School district 152 with a racial composition of 80.9% Black and 0.5% White spends $9,690 per pupil (Alliance for Excellent Education, 2009). On the national scale, research has shown that the wealthiest schools in the nation spend ten times more per pupil than some of the poorest (Meier, Kohn, Darling-Hammond, Sizer, & Wood, 2004). These funding differences can impact several aspects of the school environment, including but not limited to the school facilities, teacher and staff compensation, technological resources, support, class size, and extracurricular activities. Consequently, these differences in the relative amounts of funding per pupil has been raised as one of the factors that contributes to the test performance differences of White and Black test takers.

Tracking and Academic Rigor

Many researchers have argued that academic tracking and rigor of a school has a significant impact on the test score gap between Black and White test takers (Dauber, Alexander, & Entwisle, 1996; Kagan, 1990; Oakes, 1995). First, it has been argued that students who are placed in lower academic tracks are susceptible to a less demanding curriculum, which ultimately affects test scores and achievement. Next, some argue that some of the test performance differences can be associated with the lack of rigor in the curriculum (Darling-Hammond, 2000). For example, one indicator of rigor in curriculum is the number of Advanced Placement courses taken by students. Research has shown that minority students on average attend schools that do not offer as many advanced placement courses including those in the areas of math and science (Barton, 2003). National Center for Education Statistics (2002) reports that White students take significantly more Advanced Placement examinations in high school in comparison to Black students. As this is only one measurement of academic rigor, it still shows that there are differences in the curriculum at certain schools.

Other Factors

There are other factors that are related to the school environment that may have a more indirect effect on test performance as well. First, poor instructional leadership can impact teachers' skills and ability to teach (Wenglinsky, 2004). School safety has been found to have an effect on student achievement and consequently a student's test performance. Specifically, issues such as bullying and the presence of gangs can be an impediment to learning and academic success (Brand, Felner, Shim, Seitsinger, & Dumas, 2003; Fryer & Levitt, 2004). Studies have shown that Black students report dealing with safety issues at school almost twice as much as White students (Barton, 2003).

Teacher Factors

It has been shown that teachers have a significant effect on student achievement. As many will argue, a teacher is the primary mechanism by which students learn. Consequently, some argue that teacher-related differences are some of the most important factors that contribute to the Black White achievement gap. Therefore, it is appropriate when one is examining test performance differences to investigate the role that teachers play in the achievement of students. Presented below are several factors related to teachers that have been shown to have an impact on student achievement and test performance.

Certification and Experience

Studies have shown that teachers who have higher levels of education and are properly certified in their prospective teaching area (i.e., mathematics, English) are more effective in the classroom (Akiba, LeTendre, & Scribner, 2007; Darling-Hammond, 2000). Similarly, those teachers who have more experience and have spent more time in the classroom in comparison to novice teachers are more effective as well. In reference to the achievement gap, studies have shown that Black students are more likely to have teachers who are not certified and less experienced, while White students on average have more veteran teachers and those who have been certified in their specific area of study. Some argue that teachers' experience and certification contribute to the test performance differences of Black and White test takers.

Expectations

The next factor that has been studied pertaining to the teacher's role in test performance, is the effect that teachers' expectations of students have on achievement. Research has shown that there is a significant relationship between teacher expectations and a student's test performance. The findings show that the higher a teacher's expectation of a particular student the better the student will perform on a test (Brophy, 1983; Goodenow, 1993; Jussim, 1989; Kagan, 1990). In reference to the achievement gap, Ferguson (1998) found that teachers on average have lower expectations for Black students in comparison to White students. These differences in teacher expectations can be instrumental in perpetuating the achievement gap.

Other Factors

There are other teacher-related factors that may have an impact on achievement as well. These factors are more closely associated with resources and support of teachers and the impact those have on student achievement. First, the lack of educational materials to support instruction can affect student achievement. This particular factor can be directly related to the financial position of the school. For example, if a teacher has the equipment and materials to conduct chemistry experiments in the class, the type of experiential learning that comes with this is very different than the learning environment for those students that may only have the opportunity to read about these types of experiences in their textbook. Consequently, the differences in the types of educational materials and equipment used by teachers can impact achievement as well. Last, some argue that a teacher's level of sensitivity to cultural differences among students could have an effect on student learning and achievement (Tatum, 1997; Weiner, 2000).

Family Factors

So far, the findings presented in this chapter have focused on factors related to the school and teachers within the school. The next major component that we must examine what factors to a student's family has an effect on student achievement and test performance.

Socioeconomic Factors

Research shows that a family's income level, or socioeconomic status, has been shown to have an effect on a student's test performance (Brooks-Gunn & Duncan, 1997; Mayer, 1997). Some have argued that the Black/White test score gap is due to the fact Black families on average are poorer than White families (Phillips, Brooks-Gunn, Duncan, Klebanov, & Crane, 1998). Socioeconomic status has an effect on several of the factors previously mentioned. For instance, a family's socioeconomic status influences the schools that students attend, which affects the types of teachers they have and so on. Therefore, it is very difficult to truly discern the impact socioeconomic status has on student achievement and test performance. Although socioeconomic status can explain some of the test performance differences between White and Black test takers, it is unclear the extent to which socioeconomic status alone has on test performance (Phillips et al., 1998).

Heredity

Many have debated about the role that heredity plays in student achievement. Specifically, the extent to which heredity plays when explaining the differences in test performance between Black and White test takers. Some authors have argued that Blacks are intellectually inferior to their White counterparts, and this is the reason why we see such large differences in test performance between Black and White test takers. Most recently, the highly criticized book *The Bell Curve* (Hernstein & Murray, 1994) aimed to show that genetic differences based on racial or ethnic background can explain differences in IQ scores for Blacks and Whites. In direct opposition to this argument other researchers have shown that there is no proof that Blacks are intellectually inferior to Whites. For instance, based on his comprehensive research regarding the role of intellectual differences based on race and skin color, Nisbett (1999) states the following:

> the most relevant studies provide no evidence for the genetic superiority of either race, but strong evidence for a substantial environmental contribution to the IQ gap between blacks and whites. Almost equally important, rigorous interventions do affect IQ and cognitive skills at every stage of the life course. Moreover, the IQ difference between blacks and whites has narrowed in recent decades. The evidence thus indicates that if there are genet-

ically determined IQ differences between the races, they are too small to show up with any regularity in studies covering a wide range of populations and using a wide range of methodologies. (p. 101)

Although some studies have been aimed to show that test differences are related to race or a person's skin color, there is no evidence that these factors have an effect on test performance.

Home Environment

There are several factors related to a student's home environment that has been shown to effect achievement. First, research has shown that familial support of learning can have a significant impact on a student's academic achievement. These supportive activities can include a family's participation in school related activities or their encouragement with homework and learning outside of school. It is shown that students whose parents are involved in the school tend to have higher grades and enjoy school more. In reference to differences between Blacks and Whites in this area, research has shown that parents of minority children are far less likely to attend school events or volunteer at their children's school (Barton, 2003). Additionally, differences in the home environment, such as the amount of time kids watch television and devote to reading, can impact achievement as well (Wells, 1985). Research shows there is a significant difference in the amount of television that is watched by Black and White students, as well as a difference in the number of books in the homes of Black students in comparison to White students (National Center for Education Statistics, 2002). Specifically, the findings show that White children watch less television and have more books in the home in comparison to Black children.

Other Factors

In addition to the above factors, there are other family variables that have been examined as potential causes for differences in achievement as well. These include differences in health-related factors, such as a student's diet and nutrition, birthweight, their ability to access to health services (Brooks-Gunn, Klebanov, Duncan, 1996; Hediger, Overpeck, Ruan, & Troendle 2002; Meyers, Sampson, Weitzman, Rogers, & Kayne, 1989). These health related factors impact achievement. Research has shown that there are group differences in these factors as well.

Factors Related to the Local Community

Research has shown that there are several factors related to one's local community that can have a direct or indirect influence on students' test performance (Kober, 2001). First, the availability of economic opportunities afforded to a student's family can impact the socioeconomic status of the student's family and as stated above, have an impact on student achievement. Second, availability of adequate health care and social services can have an effect on students' educational experiences and thus their performance as well. Additional factors include but are not limited to: (a) access to libraries, museums, and other institutions that support students' development, (b) access to child care and after-school programs and facilities, and (c) community safety. Consequently, differences between these factors for Black and White test takers can be addressed as potential factors that lead to differences in test performance between groups.

Student-Centered Sources

This section focuses on factors directly related to students' own experiences and interpretations of the test environment. These issues and factors are central to the research presented in the remainder of this book. First, unlike some of the explanations that explain the achievement gap provided above, those that are related to the student have the potential to really create opportunities where interventions focused specifically on students may be available to reduce the Black and White achievement gap. Secondly, examining students in the testing environment can potentially help us to understand potential threats to the validity of the interpretation of the test scores. This is quite helpful in justifying why we should or should not use test scores for particular purposes. Presented below are some of the issues focused on the student and the test environment that have been raised to explain differences in test performance between Black and White students.

Acting White

A possible factor that has been raised to explain Black and White test score gap is in reference to Black students' perceptions of intellectual ability. Fordham and Ogbu (1986) argue that in response to Black students' doubts concerning their intellectual ability, they begin to equate academic success with being or acting White. This theory is based on the notion that certain behaviors and attitudes of minority students are criticized by their peers as acting as if they are White. For example, if a Black student received straight A's, this may be regarded by his or her peers as acting White. It has been argued that Black students' responses to achievement as being synonymous with acting White can be an explanation for why we see such differences in test performance between White and Black test takers (Cook & Ludwig, 1998).

The research that has been conducted in this area examines how academic engagement and success have been considered in minority culture as acting white. Some researchers have found that minority students may be deliberately underachieving in order to avoid social sanctions that could potentially explain the achievement gap (Fryer, 2006). Many scholars still argue about the impact that acting White has on the performance of Black students (Fryer, 2006; Jencks & Phillips, 1998). While some researchers feel this issue of acting White can explain test performance differences, others have found that it does not have an effect on test performance. Spencer, Noll, Stotzfus, and Harpalani (2001) argue that Black students' interpretation of achievement is not directly linked to the idea that their level of achievement is related to whether or not they are acting White. Although there is no consensus on the way in which the acting White theory affects Black students' test performance, it is still considered one perspective or reason to understand the Black and White achievement gap.

Stereotype Threat

Another explanation that is related to the experiences of students in the testing environment is stereotype threat. Stereotype threat is a social-psychological theory developed by Claude Steele and his colleagues that accounts for some variation in test scores and performance (Steele, Spencer, & Aronson, 2002). Stereotype threat is defined as a social-psychological threat that arises when one is in a situation or doing something for which a negative stereotype about his or her group applies. This predicament threatens an individual with being negatively stereotyped, with being judged or treated stereotypically, or with the prospect of conforming to the stereotype (Steele, 1997). When a negative stereotype about one's group becomes personally relevant, stereotype threat is the resulting sense that one's behavior or experience can be judged in terms of the stereotype. The threat is more profound for those who identify with the domain to which the stereotype applies (Steele, Spencer, & Aronson, 2002). There have been numerous studies that have investigated this phenomenon on several different tasks and tests.

Steele and Aronson (1995) investigated how stereotype threat affected Black students performance on a verbal section of the graduate record examination (GRE). The studies were performed using high-achieving (SAT-Verbal mean scores approximately 600) Stanford University undergraduates. The results showed that Black students did worse on the GRE verbal test than White participants in the high-stereotype threat condition. However, in the low-stereotype threat condition, Blacks and Whites performed equally well. Similarly, to examine the physiological effects of stereotype threat, Blascovich, Spencer, Quinn, and Steele (2001) investigated the interaction between race and stereotype threat in relation to blood pressure levels. Black and White undergraduate students were placed in either a low- or high-stereotype threat condition. In the low-stereotype threat condition, participants were told by a Black professor that they would be taking a culturally unbiased examination. Students in the high-stereotype threat condition were told by a White professor that they would be taking an intelligence test. Participants were videotaped, and their blood pressure was monitored and recorded throughout the experiment. The findings showed that Blacks in the high-stereotype threat condition performed significantly worse than Black participants in the low-stereotype threat condition on the difficult items. Moreover, Blacks susceptible to stereotype threat on a cognitive task had greater blood pressure increases than Whites. In the low-stereotype threat condition, Black and White students' blood pressures were not significantly different. The above studies are two examples of the research that has been conducted that provides evidence that stereotype threat has an effect of the standardized test performance of Black students. Figure 4.1 s a graphical depiction of stereotype threat.

This example shows how the stereotype threat affects academic achievement for a certain student. The stereotype is that Blacks students are intellectually inferior to White students in mathematics. In other words, Blacks are not as smart as Whites in mathematics. The example shows there is a Black student by the name of Ralph. Ralph is a high school junior, and he really enjoys and excels in the area of mathematics. At the end of his junior year Ralph takes the ACT. Consequently, as a result of stereotype threat, Ralph's performance on the mathematics por-tion of the ACT does not reflect his true ability in mathematics. Although

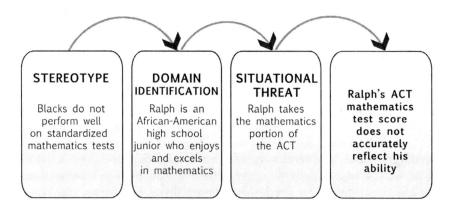

Figure 4.1.   Graphical depiction of stereotype threat.

this is definitely a very simplified way of thinking about stereotype threat, it helps one to understand the different components associated with this model. Consequently, the research done in this area has shown compelling evidence to support the idea that in relationship to particularly high-achieving Black students and standardized testing, some of the test score differences associated with standardized tests can be explained theoretically by stereotype threat.

Test Anxiety, Motivation and Self-Efficacy

Many researchers have examined how differences in test anxiety, self-efficacy and motivation affect test performance and possibly have an effect on the test performance differences of Black and White test takers (Ryan, Ryan, Arbuthnot, & Samuels, 2007). Research has shown that there is a relationship between test anxiety and test performance; as anxiety increases it shows that performance decreases (Hembree, 1988). Although several studies have examined the differences in anxiety levels of Blacks and Whites the findings are inconsistent. Some found that Blacks had higher levels of test anxiety, while others found that Whites had higher levels of anxiety (Hembree, 1988; Payne, Smith, & Payne, 1983). Nonetheless, it has been raised that differences in test anxiety could explain some of the differences in performance of Black and White test takers. Next, another explanation that has been raised in reference to Black and White test performance differences is test takers' motivation. This includes both why students are motivated to do well on the test, as well as their individual levels of to exert effort and perform on a test (Ryan, 2001; Ryan, Ryan, Arbuthnot, & Samuel, 2007). Last, differences in self-efficacy, or the belief that an individual has the ability to be successful on the task at hand, may be able to explain differences in test performance. Although there is not agreement on this topic, some research has found evidence that Black students may have lower self-efficacy in regards to how successful they feel they will be on tests (Graham, 1994).

Test-Wiseness

One factor that has been raised to explain test performance differences between Black and White test takers is the impact of one's test-taking style, or test-wiseness. Test-wiseness is defined as an individual's ability to use the testing situation to increase his/her score, independent of the construct being measured by the test (Millman, Bishop, & Ebel, 1965). Specifically, test-wiseness skills are ways in which test takers decide to skip items, use clues in the item stems, and so forth, to maximize their test score. Some evidence has shown that use of test-taking skills can improve scores 0.1 to 0.2 standard deviations (Powers, 1993). Some have argued that differences in these skills between Black and White test takers contributes to the test performance differences seen on standardized tests.

The research presented in Chapter 6 of this book examines the ways in which differences test-wiseness patterns may help to explain differences in test scores between Black and White test takers. Specifically, the research shows that White and Black test takers may differ in the way they approach tests and test items in reference to their decisions to skip test items and the amount of time they persist on test items. In reference to these specific skills, the findings show that there are significant differences in the test-wiseness patterns of Black and White test takers. Specifically, Black students' test-taking strategies are not as effective as White test takers.

Cognitive Processing

Other research has examined the way in which students process test items and how this impacts test performance differences. Specifically, the research focuses on the way in which students decide or choose how to solve particular test items and how these strategy choices may differ for White and Black test takers (Ryan, Ryan, Arbuthnot, & Samuels, 2007). Arbuthnot (2009) showed that Black students process mathematics test items differently when they are in a low-stakes test environment (i.e., classroom test) in comparison to when they are in a high-stakes test environment. This difference in the way in which Black students solve test items in the high-stakes test environment could be yet another way to understand why there are differences in test performance between White and Black test takers.

CONCLUSION

The research provided in this chapter is an overview of the explanations that have been raised to understand the achievement gap between Black and White students. As shown in this chapter, there have been a multitude of issues that have been raised, including the effects that family, school, community and individual differences have on test performance. Understanding the Black/White achievement gap has been a national concern for many years. Several researchers have contributed to understanding why we see such large differences in performance between White and Black test takers. It is clear that no one of the aforementioned sources or causes of the achievement gap can fully explain why these differences occur. However, it is advantageous for researchers to continue forging forward with research that aims to address this topic. Understanding these differences and understanding how to help all students learn has been at the forefront of the educational policy agenda. Legislation such as the No Child Left Behind Act (2002) was aimed to close the achievement gap and eliminate differences in achievement between racial groups. Other policies and programs nationwide have been geared toward understanding and diminishing this problem. New theories and explanations are important to increase our knowledge and understanding in this area.

In addition, it is important to examine these sources and explanations in order to better understand the validity of the interpretation of test scores. As outlined in Chapter 2, there are particular characteristics, content and skills that can be a threat to the validity of the interpretation of test scores. Consequently, those sources or explanations that could be regarded as a threat to the validity of the interpretation of test scores must be examined and explored. This will be instrumental in ensuring the quality of standardized tests. This leads researchers to ask the question, could this explanation of test performance differences between Black and White test takers be interpreted as a source of construct irrelevant variance? Are standardized tests measuring a characteristic, content or skill that may give one group of test-takers an advantage over another? These questions must be addressed as we continue to explore and discover potential sources that explore why there are differences between White and Black test takers. The research presented in Part II of this book is devoted to introducing new theories directly related to the student and the test environment that can help us understand the Black/White achievement gap more clearly.

CHAPTER 5

DIFFERENTIAL ITEM FUNCTIONING

INTRODUCTION

Chapter three outlined the performance differences between Black and White students on several tests, including K-12 assessments, college, graduate and professional school entrance examinations. The findings showed that there was at least a one standard deviation difference in test scores on most of these examinations. These scores are analyzed for the entire test, as well as the subtests and content areas on the examinations, such as mathematics or verbal ability. Hence, Black students are scoring significantly worse than White students on tests throughout their years of education. Many have argued that tests and test items are biased against particular populations of students, such as females and Blacks. Consequently, some believe that test and item bias can explain the differences in test performance between Black and White test takers. In response to these issues, psychometricians developed a technique called differential item functioning (DIF) to address the concern of item bias. Instead of looking solely at total test scores, DIF analyses focus on item-level differences. This chapter begins by explaining the concept of DIF. Next, it offers a discussion of the research that has been conducted in this area to understand the types of items that have traditionally shown DIF favoring

Filling in the Blanks: Standardized Testing and the Black-White Achievement Gap, pp. 47–58
Copyright © 2011 by Information Age Publishing
All rights of reproduction in any form reserved.

one group over another. The chapter then provides an overview and discussion of the proposed explanations of why certain items show DIF.

DIFFERENTIAL ITEM FUNCTIONING

There are two ways to explain differences in test performance between Black and White students. First, these differences can be explained as a result of *item impact*. Item impact is defined as a between-group difference in test performance caused by a between-group difference on a valid skill (Ackerman, 1992). These disparities may result from curricular differences or unequal exposure to a given skill. Item impact is exhibited when the item measures an actual relevant characteristic, and real differences between the two groups are found. On the other hand, differences in test performance can also be attributed to item bias. Item bias occurs when a test lacks construct validity because it contains items that measures skills other than those that it intends to measure. In an effort to understand potential sources of item bias, DIF analyses are performed. Dorans and Holland (1993) define DIF as:

> [DIF is] a psychometric difference in how an item functions for two groups. DIF refers to a difference in item performance between two comparable groups of examinees, that is, groups that are matched with respect to the construct being measured by the test. The comparison of matched or comparable groups is critical because it is important to distinguish between differences in item functioning from differences between groups. (p. 35)

Similarly, Millsap and Everson (1993) explained it as follows: An item without DIF is defined as one in which the probability of getting an item right, given a person's ability and group membership, is equal to the probability of getting an item right given a person's ability. This definition illustrates that given a person's ability level, group membership should not affect the probability of getting an item correct. Consequently, if group membership does make a difference, this item is shown to display DIF. Several methods have been developed to identify DIF on tests.

A simple illustration of DIF would be if we were to compare the performance of a group of Black students that received a 600 on the mathematics portion of the SAT with a group of White students that received a 600 on the mathematics portion of the SAT on each of the test items on the mathematics section of the SAT. For each item we would compare the probability that the group of Black students who received a 600 would get the item correct and the probability that the White students who received a 600 on the SAT would get the same item correct. We would assume that the probability for both the White and Black groups would be the same, since they all received a 600 on the mathematics portion of the SAT. However, we find items that show DIF when one group has a significantly higher probability of getting a particular item correct in comparison to the other group. Therefore in this example, we may find that on a measurement item on the SAT, White students who received a 600 on mathematics portion of the SAT had a significantly higher probability of getting this item correct in comparison to Black students who received a 600 on the mathematics portion of the SAT. This would show that the measurement test item showed DIF favoring White test takers.

The above illustration is a simplistic example of DIF analyses. In the example we were only comparing Black and White groups who received a 600 on the mathematics portion of the SAT, although this type of analysis is performed across the entire ability distribution. These analyses are conducted using several methods. These methods include, but are not limited to, the SIBTEST procedure, McDonald's method, deltaplot (TID), chi-square, and the Mantel-Haenszel procedure (Angoff, 1993).

Background on DIF

The use of DIF procedures as a means to investigate the statistical properties of a test emerged as a result of the social and political environment of the 1960s. During that period, there was a marked increase in concerns about test fairness. Since standardized testing was used for both educational and job placement purposes, many observers became apprehensive about the fairness of tests, and some people believed that they were biased against certain groups of people. During the 1970s and 1980s, there was an influx of research that addressed test bias issues. Thus, a large amount of the research in the area was published in the 1980s and early 1990s. This surge in interest in the area of DIF settled or fizzled out by the mid to late 1990s.

DIF RESEARCH

Presented below is a study-by-study review of the research that has been conducted that examines DIF comparing Black and White test takers. The research has identified content areas and other characteristics of test items that show DIF.

Black/White DIF and Math Ability

This section highlights empirical research related to DIF between Black and White test takers. The research on DIF in relation to Blacks and Whites has provided some explanations about characteristics of test items that could potentially explain why DIF exists.

Arbuthnot and Ryan (2005), examined DIF between Black and White test takers on a standardized eighth grade math assessment. The findings showed that geometry, measurement, and items including a graph or table all favored White test takers. Additionally, the study shows there are differences in motivational patterns and persistence between Black and White test takers. The research was focused on these items and did not include an examination of the items that favored Black test takers.

Scheuneman and Grima (1997) investigated characteristics of quantitative word items associated with differential performance between Black and White examinees. Using the Mantel-Haenszel procedure on quantitative reasoning items from the graduate record examination (GRE), researchers found that comparing Black and White differences in mathematics training does not play a major role in explaining DIF. The results showed that, in general, word problems were differentially harder for Black examinees. This study also found that certain characteristics of data interpretation problems showed a disadvantage to Black test takers. These included items that (a) had a large number of given values, (b) had more than one diagram, (c) involved a real setting, and (d) had a visual solution. To explain this disadvantage, researchers hypothesized that the use of data presentation in a graphic mode was less familiar to Black examinees. Data interpretation items that used money content, however, were differentially easier for Black examinees.

O'Neill and McPeek (1993) found that Blacks performed differentially better than White examinees on algebra items and items that used symbols on graduate school admissions tests. Consistent with earlier research, the authors found that word problems reflected differences between Blacks and Whites as well. Further, Blacks tended to perform better than matched White examinees on more difficult quantitative items and on pure mathematics items.

Ryan (1991) identified five items on the eighth grade Second International Mathematics Study (SIMS) mathematics that showed a moderate level of DIF. The analyses were conducted using the Mantel-Haenszel procedure. In this study, three items were found to be differentially easier for White participants. Two were classified as application items, and the other as a comprehension problem. Content-wise, two of these three items involved computation with negative numbers, while the other was a measurement item that required students to estimate a position on a ruler.

Additionally, the two items that were differentially easier for Black participants involved simple mathematical sentences and fractions.

Black/White DIF and Verbal Ability

Freedle and Kostin (1997) investigated DIF associated with GRE analogy items. Dorans and Kulick (1986) standardization technique was used to obtain DIF values. Linear regression analysis revealed that item difficulty was the best predictor of DIF variance. The results indicated that the more difficult the DIF item, the more it favored Black test takers. Items that contained words that were considered high frequency (easier) favored White students, and items with low frequency (harder) words favored Blacks. The frequency of nouns, verbs, and adjectives used in the items stems had a significant effect on the DIF associated with each problem. Lastly, items that had social-personality content favored Black test takers.

Carlton and Harris (1992) examined DIF on the SAT and the relationship between item content, such as technical or nontechnical; points tested, such as semantic relationship analogy; and format, such as math word problems. The findings showed that items containing science content favored White test takers in comparison to matched Blacks. Items that involved content related to the humanities or human relations and references to people favored Black test takers over Whites.

Scheuneman and Gerritz (1990) investigated DIF associated with reading comprehension items on the SAT and GRE. This research used the Mantel-Haenszel procedure to identify DIF items. Reading passages were analyzed with respect to the following five variables: content of the passage; demand level of the question; prepositional analysis of the stem; passage structure; and option choice. The results showed that on the GRE, 25% of the variance in Mantel-Haenszel values for Black and White test takers was related to the content of the passages. For instance, on the SAT, White examinees did differentially better on reading comprehension items dealing with narrative or science passages. This study suggests that content differences related to DIF are primarily associated with differences in prior learning, experience, and interest between Black and White examinees. In terms of item structure and test-taking style, the findings suggest that differential performance could be caused by examinees' differences in strategy choices when approaching a problem or by the way test takers respond to certain aspects of an item.

Schmitt and Dorans (1990) examined the content, format, and administration factors related to DIF on the SAT. The standardization method was used to examine DIF. The findings from the verbal section showed that Black students did differentially worse than White students on analogy items. They also found that analogy items involving homographs most frequently revealed DIF advantaging White test takers. Homographs are defined as words that are spelled like another word, but which differ in meaning or pronunciation. For this study, only items that used the less common meaning of the word were categorized as a homograph. On the other hand, items that were reported to be of interest to Black test takers were differentially easier for them. Additionally, the study found that differential speededness, or the rate at which students finished test items, also influenced DIF. Since White students finished test problems faster than Black students, this was reflected in the DIF associated with problems at the end of the test.

The research provides an overview of the types of items that have shown DIF between Black and White test takers. Tables 5.1 summarizes the findings from the DIF research.

DIF EXPLANATIONS AND SOURCES

Table 5.1 shows what types of items show DIF between Black and White test takers both related to the content (i.e., algebra, analogy) of the item, as well as the complexity (i.e., multistep, word problem) of the item. This has shed some light on the patterns of items that show DIF. However, this research does not explain *why* these differences are found. The Standards for Educational and Psychological Testing (1999) stated:

> Although DIF procedures may hold some promise for improving test quality, there has been little progress in identifying the causes or substantive themes that characterize items exhibiting DIF. That is, once items on a test have been statistically identified as functioning differently from one examinee group to another, it has been difficult to specify the reasons for the differential performance or to identify a common deficiency among the identified items. (p. 78)

The true problem arises when one starts to ask the question *why?* Why are we seeing these marked differences between matched Black and White test takers on particular items? Why do White students perform differentially better on measurement items, and Black students perform better on algebra items? What explanations can be shown to address this issue? Very often, test developers can identify items that show DIF; however, when the reason remains unexplained, the items stay on the test (Sireci, 2004) states:

> A determination of item bias requires subjective judgment that a statistical observation (i.e., DIF) is due to some aspect of an item that is irrelevant to the construct measured.... It is true many items that are flagged statistically

Table 5.1. Summarized Findings From the DIF Research

Author	Test	Items That Favor Blacks	Items That Favor Whites
O'Neill & McPeek (1993)	Math achievement test	• Algebra items • Math items containing symbols • Difficult quantitative items	
Arbuthnot & Ryan (2005)	Eighth grade mathematics achievement test		• Geometry items • Items that contain a graph or table • Measurement items • Items that require the use of estimation • Multi-step items
Ryan (1991)	Eighth grade mathematics achievement test	• Pure mathematics items • Items containing simple math sentences • Items containing fractions	• Items requiring the computation of negative numbers • Measurement item that required the use of estimation
Scheuneman & Grima (1997)	GRE: Math	• Math items that involve money	• Word problems • Math items that include a large number of given values • Items that included more than one diagram • Items that required a visual solution • Items that involved real world settings
Freedle & Kostin (1997)	GRE: Verbal	• More difficult items including: analogies, antonyms and sentence completions • Analogies that included Low frequency (i.e., harder) words • Analogies that include words that have social-personality content	• Items that included high frequency (i.e., easy) words

Table continues on next page.

Table 5.1. Continued

Author	Test	Items That Favor Blacks	Items That Favor Whites
Scheuneman & Gerritz (1990)	GRE: Verbal & SAT: Verbal		• Items based on reading passages with science content • Items based on reading passages that contained narratives
Kulick & Hu (1989)	SAT: Verbal	• Difficult verbal items	
Schmitt & Dorans (1990)	SAT: Verbal	• Items that were of interest to Black test takers	• Analogies that involved homographs • Analogy items overall
Carlton & Harris (1992)	SAT: Verbal	• Items that involved human relations, humanities and people	• Items that contain science content
Gallagher et. al (1999)[1]	Multiple tests	• Items that involved the coordinate plane • Algebra • Items that include coordinate axes	• Analogies • Items with science content • Arithmetic items • Items that involve a real world situation • Items that contain figures • Data interpretation items

1. Authors derived list of DIF items from several sources. Some of the findings were based on research from the authors that are presented above.

for DIF are never considered biased because no reason or theory can be brought forward to explain DIF. (pp. 25-26)

As stated in the above quote, the determination of item bias is quite subjective. Consequently, if there is no reason or theory known to the test developers to explain the differences found between the groups than the item would in most cases remain on the test. The research to date has identified some explanations for why DIF has occurred. One of the major reasons that has been found is that differences in one's culture has an effect on students' performance on certain test items. Next, research has found that a student's interest and experiences can affect test performance on certain items. Last, items that show DIF are sometimes simply those items that are at the end of the examination; therefore, the DIF associated with those items is merely a reflection of differential test speededness between groups. Presented below is a summary of the different explanations that have been hypothesized.

Cultural Differences

Some researchers have explained that items that show DIF are related to the content of the item. Specifically, particular items draw upon some aspect of one's culture that may or may not be central to another group's culture. Freedle and Kostin (1997) reported that some of the DIF associated with test items that they found were related to cultural differences between Black and White test takers. Freedle and Kostin stated, "We believe that the data and the background literature are in large part consistent with what we have called the cultural familiarity hypothesis in accounting for the persistent pattern of results" (p. 437)

The cultural familiarity hypothesis emphasizes the importance of culture and experience in test performance, and it argues that sociocultural context and familiarity can help to explain differential test performance between White and Black groups of examinees. For example, the results from this study showed that Blacks did differentially worse than Whites on items that involved high frequency words. The researchers suggest that cultural experiences have an effect on vocabulary usage, so common or easy words in one culture are not considered familiar or easy in another. Therefore, the different cultural environments experienced by Black and White students can influence their familiarity with certain words. Freedle and Kostin (1997) argue that cultural differences related to language and vocabulary can influence cognition. Other studies have investigated the relationship of this phenomenon to test-taking and found that culture and familiarity play a significant role in performance (Ryan, Arbuthnot, & Lin, 2002).

For example, Rogers, Dorans, and Schmidt (1986) examined DIF on the SAT-Verbal section. They found that Black students did differentially better than White students on test items that were associated with a reading passage about the achievements of a Black mathematician. This is a good example that shows how the cultural norms and differences may affect the level of DIF. This item illustrates the fact that the Black test takers could have been more familiar with the achievements of the Black mathematician in comparison to the White test takers. This issue of cultural differences in the context of the test items is typically what test developers and consumers believe is the reason why we see DIF. If that were the case the issue of DIF would be fairly easy to identify and eliminate. Unfortunately, the reasons why we see DIF on certain items is not as clear or straightforward as the item shown above. Not all DIF is necessarily related to cultural differences, as there are other explanations for these differences.

Gallagher et al. (1999) shows that an explanation of DIF could be associated specifically with cultural context. Edward T. Hall, an anthropologist, did substantial work in the area of culture. His work identified key cultural factors. Hall(1974, 1977, 1984) identified patterns of cultural context along a continuum ranging from high to low context. The research showed that minorities and females in the United States are considered high context and northern European ethnic groups and males are considered low context. Hall (1974, 1977, 1984) identified patterns of cultural context along a continuum ranging from High to Low context. Gallagher et al. (1999) identified seven major characteristics that high and low context groups differ on. The characteristics include the following: (a) interaction, (b) association, (c) temporality, (d) gender, (e) territoriality, (f) learning, (g) information, and (h) academics. The authors argue that differences based on each of these characteristics contribute to the way in which different groups of students experience test taking. Consequently, showing that cultural context can impact why we identify DIF on certain items between particular groups of test takers.

Interest and Experience

Another reason that some researchers have developed to explain DIF is related to a particular group's interest or experience with the topic or context of a test item (Schmitt & Dorans, 1997; Scheuneman & Grima, 1990). The research shows the extent to which a particular topic is of interest to a group could affect DIF. Specifically, the more interested a particular group of students is in the topic of the test item, the more likely that item will differentially favor that particular group. For example, if we are conducting a DIF study comparing males and females, and we identify a DIF item that references football and it favors male test takers, many would believe the DIF associated with that item was due the different levels of interest between males and females about football. Similarly, if there were a test item that was about flying in an airplane and it showed DIF between test takers from low socioeconomic groups and high socioeconomic groups, we would possibly conclude that the DIF was related to the test taker's experience, because we would assume that those test takers from higher socioeconomic groups may have more experience riding airplanes. Therefore, researchers have found that some DIF is associated with a test taker's interest and level of experience with the information presented in the test item.

Test-speededness. Some studies have shown that test speededness has an effect on DIF. Basically, the items positioned at the end of the test have higher DIF values favoring White test takers, because Black students tend to leave questions at the end blank more often than White students. This is not necessarily due to any aspect of the item; it is directly related to the position of the item on the test. It is assumed that if these items were positioned differently on the test, they would not show DIF. Therefore, when test developers or researchers find items that show DIF at the end of a test, they may conclude that test speededness could be the reason why these items were flagged.

Together, these explanations are helpful in understanding why certain item show DIF; however, they are definitely not showing the entire picture of what is truly happening. There are other explanations that have not been thoroughly researched that could further explain why these differences exist. As previously stated it is difficult for test developers to understand why DIF is shown on some test items. Therefore, the above explanations are not exhaustive. There are other reasons why DIF is shown on particular items. These reasons may not be related to the information presented in the item or the speed at which test takers are finishing test items, these reasons may be more closely related to the way in which different groups of test takers experience the test taking situation and how they actually process test items. Research presented in Chapter 7 in this book highlights research that examines the way in which Black students approach test items and consequently how these differences in approach can potentially impact DIF.

CONCLUSION

From a researcher's perspective, I would like to better understand why these differences are showing up and additionally develop or suggest ways to eliminate the differences. Some test developers argue that DIF doesn't make much of a difference in test score performance. Their basis for the argument is that DIF items can favor both Black and White test takers. Ultimately, they claim that the differences equal out or negate the other. Additionally, they argue that there are few DIF items that appear on tests, so they really do not make a difference. This argument to me is entirely flawed. First, from my perspective it would be quite an advantage to begin understanding why particular items show differences between groups. With a Black and White test score gap that equates to nearly a standard deviation difference in test performance, it is imperative that we examine all information that pertains to the reason that these differences exist. To truly understand Black students' test performance and to potentially help close the achievement gap, we must exhaust all our options. For example, the findings from previous DIF studies have shown that White test takers do better than matched Black test takers on geometry items. What is it about geometry items that are differentially more difficult for Black test takers? Are the differences truly based on skill or ability, or could it possibly be the way in which Black students approach geometry problems? Do Black students have a difficult time when there is a diagram or visual representation involved on a test item? If these questions can be answered in some meaningful way, then there is the possibility that teachers and practitioners would be able to address this in their curriculum and classrooms. Could it be the way geometry is taught, or, for that matter, not taught in certain classrooms? Or could it be the way particular students process items? These questions emerge to show that DIF studies are important. Yes, they may not make up a majority of the items on a particular test; however, unlocking the reasons for these differences could not only have implications on the way particular students approach certain items, but could have implications on the way particular students approach tests. DIF analyses can play a major role in uncovering the reasons for the achievement gap between Black and White students and then helping to close it. Thus, the DIF analysis is somewhat of a microanalysis of test-taking patterns. We are looking not only at test and subtest scores, but DIF looks ever closer at individual items. This microlevel examination holds a lot of promise in understanding these differences.

These explanations presented in this chapter are just scratching the surface. I believe that DIF research is not only promising, but also important to examine because it could help us to unlock some of the underlying reasons Black students perform differentially worse than White students. Although the trend of DIF research has moved on, it is important that some researchers continue to build upon this field to better understand this phenomenon. The implications of the research go well beyond just understanding the reasons for DIF. The implications of the research can move to help us understand the entire achievement gap.

PART II

BLACK STUDENTS AND
THE TESTING ENVIRONMENT

Part I provided a basic understanding of the foundational concepts regarding testing and the research that has examined sources or explanations for test performance differences between Black and White students at the test and item level. The information provided in Part I was the research that helped me to cultivate and shape my own research agenda. Now that the information has been presented to the reader, Part II of this book is my own work. The information presented in Part II reflects my perspective and understanding of the issues. Part II begins with research that I have been involved in which focuses on understanding the test-taking experiences of Black test takers in a high-stakes testing situation. This research provides new developments and ways of understanding the differences in test performance between Black and White students. Next, I will then introduce my theoretical perspective of how these differences manifest in the testing environment. These research findings are intended to not only present the new theories concerning the achievement gap, but also are supposed to challenge readers to think beyond the traditional interpretation of the achievement gap. Ultimately, these findings are intended to help readers to understand and critically evaluate the different test-taking experiences of Black and White test takers. Part II will end with recommendations and guidance provided to policymakers, researchers and academicians, and teachers.

CHAPTER 6

TEST-WISENESS

INTRODUCTION

As outlined in earlier in the book, there are several explanations and theories that have been developed to explain why we see such stark differences between the test performances of Black and White test takers on standardized tests. Although research that has been done has shown progress in understanding this phenomenon, there are yet and still other theories and explanations that may help further the discussion and consequently aid us in understanding what is most important and ultimately how we can eventually close the Black/White achievement gap.

The purpose of this chapter is to present research findings that introduce new theories or explanations that address differences in test performance patterns between Black and White test takers. Specifically, this chapter highlights two research studies that I have been involved in that examines how students' perceptions and behaviors within the testing environment have an effect on test performance differences. The chapter begins with an overview of research study that addresses how Black and White students differ in their test-taking styles and test-wiseness patterns on standardized tests. Next, the chapter highlights a study that addresses the differences in persistence patterns of Black and White students. Together these research findings illustrate how Black and White students approach the standardized testing environment differently. Ultimately showing how these differences can affect test performance and the way in which we interpret test score results.

DIFFERENCES IN TEST-TAKING STYLE AND TEST-WISENESS

Omitting and Test-Speededness Patterns

With the continued increase in the use of standardized testing, more focus has been put on students' test-taking styles. A student's success on a standardized test is due partly to his or her ability, and partly to his or her test-wiseness. As mentioned earlier, test-wiseness refers to an individual's ability to use the testing situation to increase his/her score, independent of the construct being measured by the test. Millions of dollars each year are spent on expensive test preparation courses for the SAT and many other college entrance and professional school examinations, such as the ACT, MCAT, LSAT, and GRE, among others. Indeed, some students and parents pay upward of $2,000 for preparation courses to increase test scores on the SAT, and many of these courses boast gains of nearly one standard deviation on these types of tests. For example, the *Princeton Review* course claims that *on average,* students make test score gains of 140 points on the SAT. Consequently, 140 points is a substantial score gain on the SAT. On the contrary, the College Board reports that coaching can only slightly help students on standardized tests. So, while there is disagreement about the magnitude of the score advantage for students who are coached or who take a test preparation course, there is agreement that, since the costs of these courses are sometimes substantial, there is a relative disadvantage for students who come from poor families, consequently, causing concerns that students that have the financial means to afford test preparation and/or coaching have an unfair advantage over those students who do not have the same opportunities.

Most test preparation courses focus on skills and strategies that can be useful to help students perform well on standardized tests. These test-taking skills are sometimes related to the content of the test; however, other skills, called test-wiseness skills, are related to the way in which a student approaches a test. These general and specific strategies or test-wiseness skills are used to help students maximize their test scores. Two of the strategies that are emphasized in test preparation courses are helping students understand and benefit from the directions presented on a test, as well as showing test takers how to organize their time effectively on standardized tests. Do Black and White students incorporate these strategies similarly in the testing environments? Are Black and White students using these strategies equally well in the test-taking environment?

Present Study

A research study was conducted that examined how Black and White students differ in their test-taking styles and test-wiseness patterns. In this study, a group of high school students took the SAT, a standardized test used for college admissions test. The directions stated that the test would be rights scored. This method of scoring does not penalize students for guessing. Traditionally, the SAT has been formula-scored, where there is a penalty for guessing; however, many other standardized tests, including the ACT, are rights-scored. The study then examined the frequency of students' item omissions and the number of items that a student did not reach at the end of an examination. In order to examine the omit patterns, an analysis was conducted that calculated the number of items that students skipped or omitted during the tests. This number did not include the items at the end that students were unable to answer due to time constraints. To investigate the test-speededness patterns, or the rate at which students finished the examination, an analysis was conducted of how many questions at the end of the examination the students did not reach. Consequently, the higher the number, the more items that a participant was not able to answer based on time constraints. This number was calculated for each student in the sample. Additionally, the study investigated how these patterns differed between Black and White test takers. The purpose of the research was to provide an indication of differences in test-wiseness skills between Black and White test takers, as well as differences in the way Black and White students organize their time on standardized tests.

The results showed that Black test takers omitted significantly more items than White test takers on the SAT. The finding shows that the differential omit patterns of Black and White test takers shows that there are differences in the test-wiseness skills between Black and White test takers. Consequently, since the test was a rights-scored test, it would be an advantage for test takers to guess on test items rather than skip the item entirely. In reference to test-speededness patterns, the study showed that Black students left significantly more items blank at the end of the test in comparison to White test takers. This shows that White test takers, on average, finished more test items in the time allotted for the examination. Consequently, this shows that White test takers are organizing their time more effectively in order to finish the entire test.

These findings show that test-wiseness patterns between Black and White test takers could explain some of the differences we see in test performance, since the rights-scored method of scoring an examination does not penalize students for guessing. Consequently, in order to maximize their scores, students should not skip or leave items blank when there are rights-scoring directions. From a test preparation standpoint, it is always worthwhile to answer all the questions in this type of testing scenario. This means one could be rewarded for both random guesses and educated guesses, which occur in problems in which one can eliminate some of the guesses as plausible. Hence, the study shows that White test takers have more effective test taking skills. Similarly, this leads one to believe that test preparation could help Black test takers maximize their test performance and consequently begin to close the achievement gap. This difference in test-taking behavior could be considered a reason for some of the differences we see in test performance. It still begs the question of whether standardized tests are solely measuring achievement and/or ability in a particular area or domain or is it measuring test-wiseness. Consequently, if tests are measuring test-wiseness skills in addition to the intended construct, this could point to issues related to the validity of the interpretation of test scores.

Persistence and Skipping Patterns

Arbuthnot and Ryan (2005) examined test-wiseness patterns that related the degree to which test takers persisted on items they were having difficulty with. Specifically, the research study examined the differences in persistence patterns between Black and White test takers on standardized mathematics test items. A group of Black and White eighth grade students were individually interviewed to understand how they solve standardized mathematics test items. In this study, think-aloud interviews were used to understand how students were processing standardized test items. The think-aloud accounts provided insight into what processes and knowledge the participants used during problem solving (Ericsson & Simon, 1993). Hence, think-aloud studies can be instrumental in providing a deeper understanding of the cognitive processing of individual test takers. The think-aloud protocols showed that Black students tend to persist, or spend more time on test items and tried not to skip problems. For example, a Black student attempting to solve item #15 does the following:

reads the problem
immediately reaches for calculator
keeps recalculating the problem and gets frustrated
doesn't say much while working on this problem
bites lip while continually calculating on the calculator
scratches head
chooses an option
continues to calculate

finally replies, "I can't figure it out any other way"

On the same problem, a White student attempting to solve item #15 does the following:

writes in the booklet a proportion from the calculator
gets an answer
replies, "My answer doesn't look right."
skips the problem

When comparing these two test-taking methods, it is clear that the Black student solving this problem continues to try despite having difficulties. Not only does the Black student persist on the test item, but he or she also begins to get frustrated while attempting to unsuccessfully solve the problem. On the other hand, the White student attempts to solve the item, and when the student realizes that he or she cannot solve it correctly, the student decides to move on and skip the test item. As shown by the account, the White student did not show any visual signs of frustration, while the Black student was clearly frustrated. These accounts of students' behavior while working on this item illustrate one possible difference in test-taking styles between Blacks and Whites. Specifically on timed standardized tests, when students persist too long on difficult test items, they use up valuable time they could be spending on items that they know how to solve. Second, spending excessive time on a problem that is difficult can cause frustration, which in turn can have negative effects on one's confidence and self-efficacy in taking the test. Consequently, the findings from this study showed that Black students seemed to persist longer on test items, while White students were more apt to skip and come back to items that they did not understand or felt were difficult. This difference between approaches can be seen as a possible reason for the test performance differences between Blacks and White students.

CONCLUSION

The research presented in this chapter shows that there are differences between Black and White test takers on their test-taking strategies and the way in which they approach standardized tests. The first study shows that Black and White students have different patterns of omitting test items. Specifically, Black students are skipping more items in standardizing testing situations, even when it is not advantageous for them to skip items. On the other hand, White students in this study are taking advantage of the fact that they are not penalized for guessing. This shows that White students are more sophisticated in their test-wiseness skills and are employing strategies that benefit their total test score. Additionally, this study showed that Black students are not finishing the tests as quickly as White test takers. This shows that White students are organizing their time better on standardized tests. Effective time management on standardized test is quite valuable in helping a test taker maximize their test score. Last, Arbuthnot and Ryan (2005) shows there are differences in the way in which Black and White students persist on test items on standardized tests. The findings show that White students are employing more test-wiseness skills when they are in the standardized testing environment. Some may consider this "gaming the test"; however, these test-wiseness skills can prove quite beneficial in raising one's standardized test score significantly. Further, it is important that Black students are taught how to utilize test-wiseness skills to increase their total test score.

What Does This Mean?

The findings from these studies overall show that possibly Black students' test-wiseness skills are not as well developed as their White counterparts. These differences could have an effect on total test performance, consequently, showing that test-wiseness could be another reason why we see differences in test taking. The research in this chapter focused on test-wiseness skills related to skipping, omitting, organizing time and persistence on test items; however, there are many other skills that can be taught to test takers that can help them to maximize their test score and game the test. This is more clearly recognized when we discuss coaching and test preparation for college and graduate/professional school admissions tests (i.e., SAT, MCAT, GRE). Many students spend enormous amounts of money to learn test-wiseness skills that will help them to maximize their test score and hopefully gain admittance into particular colleges and graduate/professional schools. Although many are aware of these coaching and teaching test strategies, a more fundamental question needs to be addressed. That question is, are standardized tests actually measuring the constructs they are intended to measure, or are they measuring test-wiseness skills? This can be argued from both sides, but the emphasis on the successful usage of test-taking strategies points to the fact that a test taker's ability to use test-taking strategies that may or may not be related to the construct are being measured, too. Consequently, this shows that potentially test-wiseness skills could be interpreted as a threat to the validity of the interpretation of the test scores. As previously discussed, the threat would be that test-wiseness could be interpreted as a source of construct irrelevant variance. If it is the case that test-wiseness is a source of construct irrelevant variance on a particular standardized test, what group or groups does it give an advantage to? The answer is, the group or groups that have more knowledge of and are more apt to use and apply their test-wiseness skills while taking standardized tests. The research in these studies shows that White students are using these skills much more advantageously. This shows that test-wiseness can be another reason why we see such stark differences in test performance between Black and White test takers.

CHAPTER 7

STRATEGY FORMATION AND TIME MANAGEMENT

INTRODUCTION

The book has provided information on a multitude of explanations for the differences in performance between Black and White test takers. These explanations ranged in scope. Some of the explanations focused on the students and their experiences within the testing environment itself. The purpose of this chapter is to highlight new research that has shown marked differences in the way in which Black test takers approach and experience the high-stakes standardized testing environment in comparison to a low-stakes testing environment. The findings were quite interesting and they addressed differences in the ways in which students processed and solved particular test items and the way they felt about the time constraints in the testing environment. Consequently, the findings from this research point to new directions and avenues of research that focus on Black student's strategy choices and the ways that students organize their time in high-stakes testing situation.

Filling in the Blanks: Standardized Testing and the Black-White Achievement Gap, pp. 69–75
Copyright © 2011 by Information Age Publishing
All rights of reproduction in any form reserved.

IMPACT OF TESTING ENVIRONMENT ON STRATEGY FORMATION

Arbuthnot (2009) conducted a study that explored how differences in test environments, whether their high-stakes or low-stakes, impacts mathematics standardized test performance for Black students. The research provided new insight into how the achievement gap between Black and White students becomes manifest on tests. This study helped to explain how test performance may vary by race for students of comparable abilities and how mathematical strategy choices may impact test performance differences. An experiment was conducted that randomly assigned students to a low-stakes testing environment or a high-stakes testing environment. In each condition students took a timed standardized mathematics test. In addition, follow-up interviews were conducted to gain a deeper understanding of each student's test-taking experiences and to identify the strategies that students used when approaching certain test items.

STRATEGY CHOICES

In an effort to understand strategy choices, Arbuthnot (2009) categorized students' strategies as conventional or unconventional. This categorization of strategies was based on earlier research conducted by Gallagher and De Lisi (1994). The study examined the extent to which high-achieving male and female students used different strategy choices to solve mathematics test items. In this study students took a standardized mathematics test and were asked to think aloud while solving the test items. The interviews showed what strategies the students used when approaching the mathematics test items. To examine strategy choices, the researchers classified the solutions as using either conventional or unconventional strategies. Conventional strategies were defined as solutions that use algorithms. This method for solving test items involves the use of standard computations that are typically taught in textbooks. Unconventional strategies were defined as solutions that were not typically taught in school. These solutions used some form of insight, logic, or estimation to arrive at a solution.

Arbuthnot (2009) used this strategy distinction to better understand Black students' strategy usage on a mathematics standardized test. Table 7.1. illustrates the difference between unconventional and conventional strategy choices. The examples are taken directly from the problems that were administered in the study. As can be seen, the problem asked the test taker to compare the hitting percentages for several baseball

Table 7.1.   Difference Between Unconventional and Conventional Strategy Choices

Example Problem	*Conventional Strategy*	*Unconventional Strategy*
Solve the following problem. What is 125.38 divided by 5.1? .2458 2.458 24.58 245.8	Move the decimal over one space to the right for each number in the problem. Using long division to solve: Divide 125 by 51, which is 2. 2 times 51 is 102. Subtract 102 from 125, which is 23, bring down a zero, divide 230 by 51, which is 4, 4 times 51 is 204. Subtract 204 from 230, which is 26, bring down a zero, and so on . . . until you arrive at your answer, 24.58. Answer is C.	Using estimation to solve: 5.1 is approximately 5, 125.38 is approximately 125, 125 divided by 5 is 25. Looking at the options, 25 is approximately 24.58. Answer is C.

players. Table 7.1 shows the number of hits and the total number of attempts. The conventional method of solving this test item would require the test taker to solve for the hitting percentages of each of the players (85, 81, 79, 68, and 63) and compare them. However, a test taker using an unconventional strategy would solve the problem using logic and estimation. Presented below are examples of the way in which students solving this problem approach it using both conventional and unconventional strategy choices.

Conventional Strategies

I just divided the hits made by the hits attempted, and I divide Smith 55 by 65 ... and I got 0.84, so it was 84 percent. Then Jones, I do the same thing and get 81 percent [and so on] ... so I chose A. Smith. (Danny, high-stakes condition)

When I first look, I think the answer is Smith because 55 out of 65, that's a lot. So I first divide 55 by 65 to find the percentage.... The percentage was about 85 percent for Smith. Then I went to the player that would be next highest which was ... I thought Lee ... so I divided 130 by 165 and I got 70 percent for Lee.... And I found the percentage for the rest of them and I found out that Smith ... my first thought was the correct answer [A. Smith]. (Tonya, high-stakes condition)

Unconventional Strategies

I didn't want to figure out each percentage, but I just figured out the ratio to missed the least hits. So, the top answer was 55 and 65. He only missed 10 and everybody else missed a bunch, but they also shot a lot more. Some people ... yeah, everybody shot a lot more, but he missed the least so I chose him and put A. Smith. (Andre, low-stakes condition)

I don't want to plug all the numbers in my calculator ... let me see, okay so the difference between these two [referring to Smith] was 10 and the difference between the other ones was only 10 but the difference between these two numbers was like 50 or something.... If all were more than 10 I figure the one with the least difference between the free throws attempted and free throws made was like the highest percentage, I picked A. Smith. (Mary, low-stakes condition)

As shown, Tonya and Danny, both in the high-stakes condition, used conventional strategies to solve this problem. This method required the students to conduct all of the calculations for each player and then choose the appropriate answer. Tonya's response shows that, even though her first hunch was correct, she felt it necessary to calculate all of the percentages before giving her answer. This is a fairly conservative method of arriving at an answer. On the other hand, Andre and Mary, both in the low-stakes condition, decided they did not want to perform all of the calculations, so they used logic and estimation to arrive at their answer. These examples illustrate how conventional and unconventional strategy choices differ. Although unconventional strategy choices may not always generate the correct answer, the use of these strategy choices shows a willingness to use less conservative approaches to arrive at an answer. Research has shown that using unconventional strategy choices on some problems can save time on standardized tests and reduce the risk of making errors since they require fewer calculations.

Arbuthnot (2009) found that Black students in a low-stakes testing environment used significantly more unconventional strategies in comparison to Black students in the high-stakes testing environment. The findings from this study show that students exhibited differences in the types of strategy choices used to complete the test items as a result of their testing condition. That is, being placed in a high-stakes testing environment seemed to cause Black students to approach test items with more conservative strategies (i.e., conventional) than they would in a low-stakes testing environment. Use of conservative strategy choices could consequently contribute to depressed test performance in standardized test-taking situations where there are time constraints and when test takers are presented with problems that can be more easily solved using unconventional strategy choices.

Gallagher and De Lisi (1994) state that unconventional strategy choices are particularly advantageous when approaching certain test items. Based on their research we assume that the testing environment in and of itself forces Black students to approach problems differently than if they were not in a standardized testing situation. Could this difference in approach be detrimental to their overall test score and experience? It seems that this could be a plausible reason why we see some differences in test performance. Understanding the cognitive processes that Black students undertake in the testing environment is crucial in helping to understand ways in which we can help Black students perform well in the testing environment. If one of the reasons we see these differences in test performance between White and Black students can be attributed to strategy formation, we can help teachers encourage Black students to use nontraditional or unconventional test strategies in the high-stakes testing environment.

IMPACT OF TEST ENVIRONMENT ON STUDENT'S TIME MANAGEMENT AND ORGANIZATION

In addition to investigating the effects that the testing environment had on strategy choices, Arbuthnot (2009) also examined the effect that test environment had on the way in which Black students organize their time while taking a standardized test. Interviews with students from both the high-stakes and low-stakes testing condition revealed interesting findings about the differences in the way Black students felt about time constraints and how they organized their time while taking the standardized test. The findings showed that participants in the high-stakes condition reported having significantly more problems dealing with the time constraints of the test in comparison to students in the low-stakes condition. Forty percent of the students in the high-stakes condition mentioned feeling pressure about running out of time or having to rush at the end of the standardized test, while, none of the students in the low-stakes condition reported having these difficulties. Presented below are excerpts from the interviews that illustrate how students reported issues related to time constraints.

Then I noticed time was running out, so I could make sure that I could get the next one done and come back to this one, and I read it again and read it again, but finally I just gave that answer. (Lonnie, high-stakes condition)

I rushed through this one [Why?] It was just like annoying, so I really didn't think about it, and I just rushed through it. If I had more time, I would have went through the whole thing. (Kevin, high-stakes condition)

I just tried to hurry up…. I wanted to hurry up. (Antwon, high-stakes condition)

Implications of the Research

The studies conducted by Arbuthnot (2009) show that the testing environment itself has an impact on the way Black students experience and perform on standardized tests. The experiment conducted shows that merely changing the standardized testing environment (i.e., low-stakes/high-stakes) can have a significant effect on Black students' strategic approach and time organization skills. These differences illuminate the fact that one must be mindful of these issues when interpreting the results of standardized tests. One must ask the question: Are standardized tests a valid indicator of test performance? There is an ongoing debate concerning the validity of the interpretation of test scores. The ultimate question is, can we have confidence that scores on standardized tests are an accurate portrayal of one's ability in a particular domain. This research illuminates the fact that just simply changing the intent or purpose of a test can drastically change the ways in which Black students approach standardized tests.

CONCLUSION

The research and theories presented in this chapter based on Arbuthnot (2009) show how Black and White students may differ in how they approach standardized testing. The findings could have an effect on educational theory, policy and practice. Providing evidence that shows the different ways students approach the high-stakes testing environment provides a significant contribution to educational theory. This research could help test developers and educational researchers understand and interpret test performance differences more clearly. This research is also important to educational practice because it provides educators and administrators a more refined understanding of the test-taking experiences and patterns Black students. Specifically, it highlights the need for educators (i.e., teachers, administrators) to be aware of the social and psychological factors that contribute to or impair high-achieving Black students' standardized test performance. Recognizing the ways in which Black students perform in the high-stakes testing situation can prove to be beneficial in assisting educators in developing interventions that will help them approach test items differently. Given the emphasis of standardized testing in the No Child Left Behind Act (2002), it is imperative that researchers investigate potential threats to the validity of the interpretation of test scores and present these findings to the public. Studies such as this one could ultimately shape future educational policy by assisting legislators in making informed decisions about the possible limitations of using standardized assessment as the sole basis for accountability.

CHAPTER 8

COGNITIVE PROCESSING

INTRODUCTION

The research presented in Part I of this book shows the large differences in test performance between Black and White test takers on several standardized tests. After seeing such large differences in group performance, we naturally assume that one group is deficient in a certain academic area or in several areas. For instance, in mathematics, the largest gaps in this area are on items that assess Measurement. Therefore, we believe that Black students lack the abilities or skills required to excel on these types of items. However, based on the research presented in Chapter 7, could the explanation be that if Black students were given these tests items in a low-stakes testing environment, they could perform the same tasks better than they could in the high-stakes environment? In other words, is the environment itself a potential factor that may be measured in the high stakes test environment in addition to students' skills?

The research in Chapter 7 shows that when Black students are in the low-stakes environment, they perform significantly better on mathematics test items and used more unconventional testing strategies when approaching test items. How do these differences manifest themselves in the testing environment? One way to understand their dilemma in the testing environment is to ask what happens to Black students when they are put in this high-stakes environment? When Black students do not feel safe in the testing environment, they choose safe test-taking strategies. Why do their strategies change, based on environment?

Black Students

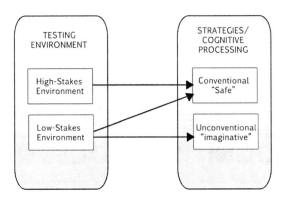

White Students

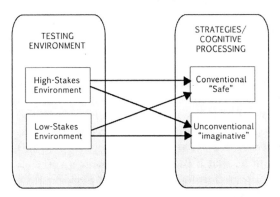

Figure 8.1.   The options that Black and White students have in the low-stakes and high-stakes testing environment

Figure 8.1 above illustrates the options that Black and White students have in the low-stakes and high-stakes testing environment. As can be seen in Figure 8.1, Black test-takers on standardized mathematics tests typically have one option in the high-stakes testing situation. That option is to solve items more conservatively, using conventional strategies. However, when the Black test takers are put in a low-stakes testing environment, their choices change. They feel more comfortable choosing either the conventional or the unconventional, more imaginative strategies. In contrast, as illustrated in Figure 8.1, White students on standardized mathematics tests have the options of using both conventional and unconventional strategies in the low- and high-stakes testing situations. Why do we see these differences in the ways in which particular groups solve items in the testing environment? What makes Black test takers feel that they have to approach the test differently in a high- or low-stakes environment?

COST BENEFIT

One perspective that can explain why these differences can occur is directly related to the financial concept of cost benefit. In the area of finance, a cost benefit analysis is used to assess the relative costs and benefits of a particular project or decision. A cost benefit analysis is defined as a method of weighing the total expected benefits from the total expected cost of a particular decision. Cost benefit analyses are conducted for both governmental and private sector decision making. The process involves placing a value on the benefits of a particular decision in reference to the actual costs. The accuracy of the cost benefit analysis is based on the assumption that the costs and benefits have been properly estimated. Research shows that this type of analysis is done explicitly and implicitly, and many people conduct cost benefit analyses informally when making everyday decisions.

For instance, when driving to work, one may conduct an informal cost benefit analysis when making the decision to take the highway or the city streets. In this example, the decision is based on the costs and the benefits associated with each option. Consequently, on a normal day, taking the highway is the easiest and fastest route to and from work; however, oftentimes a small accident will create additional traffic and most likely cause the trip to be significantly longer. On the other hand, taking the streets to work is longer on average; however, there are rarely any accidents along this route, so one does not have to worry about any added time. Based on this scenario, one will choose the costs and benefits associated with each route to determine which way to take to and from work. The choice of route will change based on particular circumstances. For example, when there is a mandatory meeting at work, one may decide to take the streets to work. Although taking the streets to work is the longer route, it is still the most dependable and reliable; therefore, you can be assured you arrive at work on time to make the meeting. However, if you are leaving work and want to rush to go home and watch your favorite television show, you may decide to take the highway with the hope that there are no accidents. This is based on the notion that if you do run into an accident, the only costs associated with getting home late is that you miss your favorite television show. The above example is an illustration of how one conducts cost benefit analyses in their everyday lives.

A cost benefit analysis can be used to understand standardized testing environments and how different groups experience testing situations. For instance, a cost benefit analysis can be applied to understand the ways in which particular students make choices concerning which strategy to use on particular test items. As reported in Chapter 7, when students approach a test item, they must decide what type of strategy they will use to solve the test item. On mathematics items that have multiple solutions to solve, students are faced with a decision of which strategy they should use to solve the particular test item. At this point, they must make a decision. They recognize there is more than one method to solve this test item, so they informally conduct a cost benefit analysis. The questions arise, what are the costs associated with choosing each method? and what are the benefits in choosing each method? They must assess what the costs and benefits are to answering this item each of the different ways. One method of solving the item is the conventional method, and the other is the unconventional method (as described in Chapter 7). The test taker must decide what costs and benefits are associated with each method. Based on the research found in this area, the costs and benefits of using more unconventional strategy choices change based on context as well as across groups. What are the costs and benefits of using the different methods of solving the test items in the high- and low-stakes testing environment? Tables 8.1 and 8.2 provide the costs and benefits for Black and White students using an unconventional or conventional strategy choice in a high-stakes and low-stakes environment.

Comparison Across Testing Situation

As can be seen in Tables 8.1 and 8.2, the costs and benefits associated with each strategy choice addresses issues that are related to the following: (a) points on the test, (b) influence on total test performance, (c) effects of performance, (d) time spent on test item, and (e) accuracy. For Black test takers, the findings presented in Tables 8.1a and 8.1b show that all of the costs and benefits associated with the high-stakes and low-stakes test are consistent except for three. The three issues that are not consistent across test situation are the effects the test performance will have on a student's school; a student's group (i.e., race, gender); and the high-stakes criteria, such as high school graduation or grade promotion. This is consistent with the findings for White students presented in Tables 8.2a and 8.2b.

As previously stated, in the low-stakes test environment, Black students are more prone to use unconventional strategy choices, which mean that the benefits outweigh the costs when they are given an opportunity to solve items in this manner. On the contrary, in the high-stakes environment, research has found that Black test takers choose to use more conventional strategy choices. Consequently, the cost benefit analysis shows that the costs of using an unconventional strategy choice outweigh the benefits; therefore, Black students choose not to use the unconventional

Table 8.1a.   Black Students in a High-Stakes Testing Environment

	Cost	*Benefit*
Conventional Strategies	• Lose a point on the test. • Negative influence on my total test performance. • Worry about accuracy when solving test item. • Additional time spent on solving test item. • Performance affects the following: 1. Me 2. My school 3. My group and my group has traditionally performed poorly. 4. High-stakes decision (i.e., graduation, grade promotion).	• Additional point on the test. • Positive influence on my total test performance. • Performance affects the following: 1. Me 2. My school 3. My group and my group has traditionally performed poorly. 4. High-stakes decision (i.e., graduation, grade promotion).
Unconventional Strategies	• Lose a point on the total test. • Negative influence on my total test performance. • Performance affects the following: 1. Me 2. My school 3. My group and my group has traditionally performed poorly. 4. High-stakes decision (i.e., graduation, grade promotion).	• Additional point on the test • Saved time • Did not have to worry about accuracy compared to solving it in the conventional manner. • Positive influence on my total test performance. • Performance affects the following: 1. Me 2. My school 3. My group and my group has traditionally performed poorly. 4. High-stakes decision (i.e., graduation, grade promotion).

Table 8.1b Black Students in a Low-Stakes Testing Environment

	Cost	*Benefit*
Conventional Strategies	• Lose a point on the test. • Negative influence on my total test performance. • Worry about accuracy when solving test item. • Additional time spent on solving test item. • Performance affects the following: 1. Me	• Additional point on the test. • Positive influence on my total test performance. • Performance affects the following: 1. Me
Unconventional Strategies	• Lose a point on the total test. • Negative influence on my total test performance. • Performance affects the following: 1. Me	• Additional point on the test • Saved time • Did not have to worry about accuracy compared to solving it in the conventional manner. • Positive influence on my total test performance. • Performance affects the following: 1. Me

strategy choices in the high-stakes testing environment. Based on these findings, we can see in Table 8.1 that the additional three issues that are raised (the effect their test performance will have on the student's school, the student's group (i.e., race, gender), or the high stakes criteria) in the high-stakes environment increase the costs associated with using the unconventional strategies. This causes Black students to decide not to use unconventional strategies very often, because the costs of getting an item incorrect using this method outweighs the benefits of using the method.

Black students' strategies change because the opportunity costs change. What is the cost of getting an item wrong? Who is affected? Black students are affected, and it is a reflection of not only the individual students, but their school and their race, so the cost is much higher. Therefore, it is easy to understand why the differences are much smaller on items that are more formulaic like algebra because they can directly solve the item. However, when there is a choice involved, the dilemma returns. They ask themselves, "What solution or strategy do I use?" Items that have multiple solutions cause students to make a choice, and the choice is not necessarily, "Can I solve it?" but "Which way do I solve it?" In other words, students wonder, "Do I choose the solution path that would save me time and essentially effort, or do I take the solution path that is more straightforward and more time consuming?"

As discussed, when Black students weigh the costs associated with choosing a strategy choice they tend to choose the safe or more conservative solution. Although students choose the conservative solution does not mean that the student does not have the aptitude to know that there is another solution that may be more unconventional and save them time. Most likely, they do know there is another method; however, they

Table 8.2a.   White Students in a High-Stakes Testing Environment

	Cost	*Benefit*
Conventional Strategies	• Lose a point on the test. • Negative influence on my total test performance. • Worry about accuracy when solving test item. • Additional time spent on solving test item. • Performance affects the following: 1. Me 2. My school 3. My group, and my group has traditionally performed well. 4. High-stakes decision (i.e., graduation, grade promotion).	• Additional point on the test. • Positive influence on my total test performance. • Performance affects the following: 1. Me 2. My school 3. My group, and my group has traditionally performed well. 4. High-stakes decision (i.e., graduation, grade promotion).
Unconventional Strategies	• Lose a point on the total test. • Negative influence on my total test performance. • Performance affects the following: 1. Me 2. My school 3. My group, and my group has traditionally performed well. 4. High-stakes decision (i.e., graduation, grade promotion).	• Additional point on the test • Saved time • Did not have to worry about accuracy compared to solving it in the conventional manner. • Positive influence on my total test performance. • Performance affects the following: 1. Me 2. My school 3. My group, and my group has traditionally performed well. 4. High-stakes decision (i.e., graduation, grade promotion).

Table 8.2b.   White Students in a Low-Stakes Testing Environment

	Cost	Benefit
Conventional Strategies	• Lose a point on the test. • Negative influence on my total test performance. • Worry about accuracy when solving test item. • Additional time spent on solving test item. • Performance affects the following: 1. Me	• Additional point on the test. • Positive influence on my total test performance. • Performance affects the following: 1. Me
Unconventional Strategies	• Lose a point on the total test. • Negative influence on my total test performance. • Performance affects the following: 1. Me	• Additional point on the test • Saved time • Did not have to worry about accuracy compared to solving it in the conventional manner. • Positive influence on my total test performance. • Performance affects the following: 1. Me

choose the safe option because in the testing environment, the cost is too high. Consequently, the assumption that particular groups of students have cognitive difficulty with these types of items is not necessarily true. The truth could be that because of the present situation—the high stakes environment—they have chosen to solve it in a different way, but this does not imply that they do not have the ability to solve it in other ways.

Comparisons Across Race

Tables 8.1 and 8.2 compares the cost and benefits of using different strategies for Black (Table 8.1) and White (Table 8.2) test takers in a low- and high-stakes testing environment. for Black and White test takers in a low- and high-stakes testing environment. As can be seen in both figures, the costs and benefits associated with each testing environment addresses issues related to the following: (a) points on the test, (b) influence on total test performance, (c) effects of performance, (d) time spent on particular items, (e) accuracy issues. Making comparisons between the tables for the Black (8.1) and White (8.2) test takers we see a difference in the components of the costs and benefits in the high-stakes environment. Specifically, we see all of the components of costs and benefits related to using unconventional strategy choices are consistent between Black and White test takers except for one. The only difference between the cost and benefits between Black and White test takers is the effect the total test performance will have on his or her respective group. The issue arises particularly when we examine the differences in the high-stakes testing environment.

What could possibly explain why White students and Black students differ in their assessment of the costs and benefits of the effects their test performance has on their respective racial group? One explanation of this could be strictly cultural. Presented in Chapter 5 is a brief overview of how cultural context differs for high context groups versus low context groups. As discussed, Hall (1974) identified ethnic minorities and females in the United States as high context groups, while northern European ethnic groups, including White males, were categorized as low context groups. These groups were distinguished on several characteristics, such as academics, learning, and interaction with others. One characteristic that may be instrumental in helping to explain the differences in the ways in which Black and White students assess the costs and benefits associated with the effects of their performance to the group is the cultural differences in the way in which the different groups associate with others. Specifically, Hall (1974, 1977, 1984) found that low context groups feel that their personal commitment to other people is low, while high context groups feel that their personal commitment to other people is high. Consequently, the differences in the way low and high context view their commitment to others can have an effect on the way in which they weigh the costs or the benefits in how their performance affects the group as a whole. Thus, the high context groups may believe that there is a higher cost and higher benefit to ensuring that they perform well for the group; whereas the low context group does not put as much weight on the idea that their individual performances will affect the whole group's performance. Consequently, this can affect the ways in which Blacks and Whites assess which type of strategy to solve particular test items. Specifically, this shows that if Black students, who are considered high context culturally, assess the cost and benefits of their test performance they address the way in which their performance, would affect the group as a whole. On the other hand, for White males, who have been shown to have a low cultural context, when they assess the costs and benefits of their strategy choices they may not care as much that their test performance will affect the larger group. This differential understanding of the impact that one's test performance will have on others could significantly affect the way in which different groups approach test taking and the way they choose to solve test items.

Going back to the example presented earlier in this chapter that discussed one's decision to decide which route to choose to go to work, what if the cost of getting to work on time didn't affect just you individually, but had an effect on your entire department at work. This would have a great impact on the costs and benefits of taking the short cut route or taking the longer safer route, because in this example it would no longer benefit just you to get to work on time, but it would benefit you and your department. This would have a significant effect on your decision making. Consequently, no longer making your decision simply a personal decision, it would now be looked at as a decision that would impact your entire department at work. This would make the cost and benefits even more crucial if you felt that the group or your team at work was important to you. As we see from this example, the addition of the group dynamic makes the decision much more clear and straightforward. Since the costs and benefits have changed, I must be sure to take the safe, more reliable route to work. This is what Black students have to contend with in the testing environment. They are weighing the costs and benefits of their performance, and deciding that the costs and benefits are high enough for them to decide to take the safe route. However, taking the safe route on a standardized test is not always advantageous. It puts test takers at a disadvantage when there are clearly easier and simpler methods of solving particular problems. Unfortunately, for Black students, the costs associated with using these other methods that involve skipping steps or approximating, to arrive at an answer, are too high.

Accuracy of Cost Benefit Analysis

As previously discussed, the accuracy of the cost benefit analysis is based on the assumption that both the costs and benefits have both been estimated accurately (Flyvbjerg, Bruzelius, & Rothengatter, 2003; Flyvbjerg, Holm, & Buhl, 2002). Are Black students accurate in their assessment of the costs and benefits associated with using unconventional strategies in each of the testing environment? Comparing Black and White students in a high-stakes situation, it seems that Black students are assessing that using an unconventional strategy choice and answering the test item incorrectly demands a higher cost than the corresponding benefit of using an unconventional strategy choice and getting a correct answer. As can be seen in the above sections, Blacks students could potentially underestimate the benefits of using unconventional strategies or overestimate the costs associated with this method of problem solving in comparison to White students. This shows that further research needs to be focused on understanding the way in which Black students operate and make decisions in a test-taking situation. If our ultimate objective is to help students show what they know, we need to better understand the mechanisms that they attend to in the testing situations and the ways in which they make decisions that can affect the validity of the interpretation of their test scores. Most interesting is to understand that these decision processes are different across the testing environment and across groups. Understanding why these differences are present could be helpful in helping Black students in particular maximize their test performance on tests in high-stakes testing environments.

COGNITIVE PROCESSING AND OTHER ACADEMIC AREAS

Arbuthnot (2009) shows that in the area of mathematics, Blacks tend to be more conservative in their strategy choices when taking a high-stakes test; however, when Black students are in a low-stakes testing environment, they have more versatility in the ways in which they solve mathematics test items. Specifically, they are more apt to use both conventional and unconventional strategy choices. The question is, can this information about strategy choices be translated into other academic areas? Although the research in this area has been focused primarily on mathematics, these same concepts can be applied to other academic areas. For example, research has shown that there are large differences in performance between Black and White students on verbal ability tests. More specifically, research has shown that Analogy test items favor White test takers in comparison to matched Black test takers. To understand if strategy choices could help to explain test performance differences, we must examine the components of analogies.

Analogy questions are included on several standardized tests. For instance, the graduate record examination (GRE) created by the Educational Testing Service contains analogies. Educational Testing Service (2002) provides a detailed explanation of an Analogy item on the GRE (see Figure 8.2).

As stated in Figure 8.2, a GRE analogy problem tests one's ability to recognize the relationship between two pairs of words. It continues to say that on occasion, the answer choices to the analogy items includes multiple pairs of items that may seem to express a relationship similar to the sample pair in the question; however, there is one relationship that is more precise. Based on the information provided in the description of the analogy problem, we can see that on some items there is the possibility that more than one solution is plausible. Consequently, there could be more than one solution that is correct; however, the correct answer is the one that is most precise. In terms of the information that we learned about strategy choices in mathematics, how can this relate to analogy items?

The explanation for the Analogy question type appears below followed by the directions for the sample Analogy questions.

Analogy questions test your ability to recognize the relationship between the words in a word pair and to recognize when two word pairs display parallel relationships. To answer an Analogy question, you must formulate the relationship between the words in the given word pair and then select the answer containing words related to one another in most nearly the same way. Some examples are relationships of kind, size, spatial contiguity, or degree.

Here are some approaches that may be helpful in answering Analogy questions:

- Before looking at the answer choices, try to establish a precise relationship between the words in the given pair. It is usually helpful to express that relationship in a phrase or sentence. Then look for the answer choice containing the word pair whose relationship is closest to that of the given pair and can be expressed in a similar fashion.

- Occasionally, more than one of the answer choices may seem to express a relationship similar to that of the given pair. Try to state the relationship more precisely, or identify some aspect of the relationship that is paralleled in only *one* choice pair.

- Remember that a single word can have several different meanings. Check to be sure you have not overlooked a possible second meaning for one of the words.

- *Never* decide on the best answer without reading *all* the answer choices.

- Practice recognizing and formulating relationships between word pairs.

Figure 8.2.   Explanation of an Analogy item on the GRE.

One major issue is that, as stated in the directions, there are problems that have essentially multiple solutions. Gallagher et al. (2000) showed that test items that have multiple solutions to solve were considered to be unconventional. Instead of examining the actual strategy choices used to solve math problems, the authors in this study examined the items themselves and categorized each item as being a conventional or an unconventional item. The research showed that items that have multiple solutions were categorized as being unconventional in nature. Additionally, the authors found in the area of mathematics, females had a more difficult time on items that had potentially multiple solutions. The problem becomes one of judgment, deciding upon the better solution of the two. This relates to the information presented earlier in the chapter concerning the ways in which students have to make decisions about choosing which solution to solve the problem or which is essentially a better way.

It would seem plausible to say that those Analogy items that have been shown to have multiple solutions would be particularly problematic to Black test takers. Based on the research that was conducted in mathematics, those unconventional problems that can be solved in multiple ways present Black students and females with a dilemma. Unlike other problems that have a more definitive solution, these types of problems make students second guess themselves and have less confidence about their answering and problem-solving ability. This is particularly problematic for a Black student whose costs and benefits associated with their test performance are much higher on the examination than the cost benefit on the same test would be for others. It is possible that if given the same analogy problems in a low-stakes environment, Black students would no longer have the same issues to contend with and therefore may be more comfortable and confident when formulating an answer on analogy items that have multiple solutions.

Further research needs to be conducted examining the ways in which Black students approach unconventional items. This research can be instrumental in helping to understand testing patterns in academic areas other than mathematics. As presented above, we can see how some analogy problems could be categorized as being unconventional. This helps us to further understand some of the larger differences found on standardized tests. It would be interesting to conduct studies that examine this issue in other academic areas such as science, where we see the large gaps as well.

CONCLUSION

The purpose of this chapter is to provide an overview of issues related to cognitive processing and test performance. Specifically, the chapter focuses on presenting explanations and ideas related to why there are differences in the ways in which Black and White test takers approach and process test items. These explanations include an understanding of how students assess the costs and benefits associated with using certain test strategies, and provide connections between research that addresses cognitive processing of mathematical items and applying those same findings to other academic areas.

The notion that the costs and benefits related to standardized tests are different for certain groups brings up a very important point. The point is that beyond the information on the test, our culture and values can affect the way we approach a particular situation and the value placed on that situation, more importantly, our interpretation of who and what will be directly affected by our actions. As presented earlier in this chapter, Black students tend to have a different perception of the cost and benefits associated with their standardized test performance. Consequently, their test performance is no longer a personal journey, but one that affects not only them, but their school, parents and their racial group as a whole. Given this information we can see that in recent years the emphasis of the No Child Left Behind Act (2002) to disaggregate test performance by group exacerbates this notion of group consciousness. The fact that Black students are traditionally at the bottom of the spectrum on standardized tests and the rewards and sanctions are based on group performance, we see how this could have a profound effect on Black student performance. Specifically, at the microlevel, we see the effects of Black students' interpretation of the cost and benefits of using particular strategy choices to solve test items and their interpretation of their performance on the test.

Understanding that these differences occur in the test taking environment are important. Being able to disentangle the differences in the testing experience between Black and White test takers can help further the dialogue of why we see these distinct differences in test performance. As I have mentioned, all the reasons or explanations for differences are not always directly related to what a student knows; it is sometimes related to the way in which they approach the situation. What seems to be most important in regards to standardized tests is the notion that all students are able to show what they know. If Black students are approaching standardized tests in ways that limit their strategy usage, are they truly showing what they know? Undoubtedly, the answer to this question is no. Black students who limit their strategy choices are not truly showing what they know, particularly if they would be able to perform differently if the testing conditions were changed (i.e., low-stakes). Of the greatest importance is that since we have established the different ways that groups approach standardized test items, we may begin the dialogue of what can be done to help. Unfortunately, if we don't know and don't understand the experiences of particular groups in the test situation, we cannot make real strides in helping to make changes in closing the gaps. Further research should be focused on gaining a deeper understanding of how Black and White students differ in the way in which they process test items. These differences can be helpful in understanding some of the test performance patterns.

CHAPTER 9

GUIDANCE FOR STAKEHOLDERS

INTRODUCTION

Our current educational accountability system is based on the use of standardized tests. The chapters in this book were presented to help readers understand the standardized tests and the Black-White achievement gap more clearly. Standardized tests have the potential to be very valuable in providing useful information to understand patterns of achievement. However, it is imperative that we use testing data in ways that will be beneficial to our educational system and have a positive effect on educational outcomes for all students. Very often, many assume that a test score alone will provide sufficient information that will gauge a student's ability or achievement in a particular domain. It is of utmost importance that educational policymakers are aware of the limitations that exist using standardized tests.

The purpose of this chapter is to provide suggestions, recommendations and insight to policymakers, researchers, academicians and teachers and government officials, researchers/academicians, and practitioners/teachers regarding the use of standardized tests and the different ways to understand test performance differences between Black and White test takers. The information provided is based on my educational experiences

Filling In the Blanks: Understanding Standardized Testing and the Black/White Test Score Gap, pp. 91–121
Copyright © 2011 by Information Age Publishing

both in and out of the classroom, as well as research that has helped to enlighten my understanding of standardized testing and the Black-White achievement gap.

POLICYMAKERS

Threats to Validity

Chapter 2 in this book outlined two major areas that can be seen as potential threats to the validity of the interpretation of test scores, which include construct underrepresentation and construct irrelevant variance. The recommendations concerning validity issues will be focused on the latter, construct irrelevant variance. As stated, construct irrelevant variance is present when a test measures skills or characteristics that are not directly related to the construct being measured. The research presented in this book examines patterns of difference between Black and White test takers, as well as the impact of test environment on test performance. Some of the issues that were addressed are those related to differences in test-wiseness patterns between Black and White test takers, such as persistence and organization of time and the ways in which Black students approach the high-stakes testing situation differently than they do a low-stakes testing situation. In general, both of these findings could constitute concern about the validity of the interpretation of test scores. For instance, if Black students are approaching the high-stakes testing situation differently than they were in a low-stakes situation, this could lead one to believe that the testing situation or environment, particularly for Black test takers, is being measured in addition to the stated construct of the test. The argument is even stronger when we compare the performance of this same group in a low-stakes situation and their performance changes. This shows that the testing environment for Black students could be seen as a source of construct irrelevant variance. Similarly, the differences in test-wiseness patterns and the subsequent impact on test performance could be a concern as well, thus making the argument that tests could be measuring test-wiseness skills in addition to the construct it was intended to measure (i.e., mathematical achievement).

Based on this information, it is imperative that educational policies which are centered on standardized tests must take into consideration the validity issues regarding the interpretation of test scores. It is equally important that policymakers understand the differing experiences of particular groups of test takers and the effects standardized tests have on each group.

Accountability Measures for Test Developers

The major educational emphasis in our country over the last decade has been accountability. The No Child Left Behind (NCLB) Act (2002), as well as other educational policies, have highlighted the need for accountability. The accountability issues have focused on states, schools, administrators and teachers. The policies have outlined ways that each of these stakeholders have to become more accountable for students' learning and their subsequent learning outcomes. In fact, NCLB actively sanctions those stakeholders who are not meeting standards. Therefore, in this same spirit, test developers should be held accountable for their products, such as standardized tests which claim to measure particular constructs. Indeed, if we are going to hold the aforementioned stakeholders accountable for their efforts in helping to increase student achievement, we must, in turn, hold test developers accountable for the measurement that we use to assess student achievement. This type of accountability is needed and necessary, especially given the increased emphasis that has been placed on standardized tests.

At present, there is no oversight board or committee whose responsibility is to regulate or oversee the construction and use of standardized tests (Zwick, 2002). With such an emphasis on test scores and the high-stakes involved with these tests, it is important to have some oversight for this industry. The products and tests that are produced through the testing industry have high-stakes consequences for students, including student retention, dropout rates, and basically the career and educational trajectories of most students. It is imperative that there exist some type of oversight committee that would govern or audit what the test developers and state agencies are producing and using to gauge student success.

The Standards of Educational and Psychological Testing (1999) were established to provide guidance for test developers to follow. These standards outline what issues and concerns test developers should follow in order to ensure high quality assessments. How do we ensure that these issues related to reliability, validity and fairness are being addressed? If there is accountability for schools and teachers, there needs to be accountability for test developers, as well. Millions of dollars are being funneled into the testing industry from local and state governments and from the federal government to develop tests to be used for multiple purposes, including grade level tests, grade promotion tests, and high school graduation exams. With the consequences of these tests being so high, it is policymakers' responsibility to ensure there is some form of audit or oversight pertaining to test developers.

The State Board of Education of a western state within the United States contracted with a test developer to construct and score their reading, language, and mathematics assessment for the K-12 students. This test was used to meet reporting requirements of the NCLB (2002). A research study was conducted that examined the DIF patterns on this assessment. As previously discussed in Chapter 5, differential item functioning (DIF) analyses are conducted to detect items that could potentially be biased toward one group in comparison to another. In this study, the DIF analyses compared White and Hispanic test takers, in addition to gender differences. The findings showed that 7% to 19% of the items on some of the tests examined showed DIF between racial/ethnic groups. Surprisingly, 7% to 37% of the items on some of the examinations showed DIF between males and females.

The results of this study raise concerns. The fact that there were as much as 19% of the items on a test that showed racial/ethnic DIF and up to 37% of the items on a test showed gender DIF is particularly problematic. This is quite a large percentage of items on the test that could have the potential to be biased against a certain group of test takers. The Standards of Educational and Psychological Testing (1999) state in Standard 7.3:

> When credible research reports that differential item functioning exists across age, gender, racial/ethnic, cultural, disability, and/or linguistic groups in the population of test takers in the content domain measured by the test, test developers should conduct appropriate studies when feasible. Such research should seek to detect and eliminate aspects of the test design, content, and format that might bias test scores for particular groups.

Based on the information provided by this standard, it is important in the test development process to conduct DIF studies. The test developer who constructed this test either did not conduct studies to detect DIF on this test, or conducted the DIF analysis and did not eliminate any or enough of the items that showed moderate to large DIF. This example clearly shows why it is important to have some form of auditing or oversight committee for test developers. This type of policy or legislation will ensure that standardized tests, which are used for high-stakes decisions, have been studied and scrutinized to ensure that the tests are of high quality and are fair to all members of the test-taking population.

Teacher Interventions

Testing has become the cornerstone of our nation's educational reform system. NCLB (2002) utilizes standardized tests as a means to hold states accountable for the education of all students. It has become apparent that many school personnel do not thoroughly understand the nature of testing. While there is real concern for raising test scores, many teachers and administrators lack the expertise and training needed to understand how to use student achievement data to increase student learning. In a speech at Columbia University's Teacher's College, Arne Duncan, United States Secretary of Education, stated that there were two issues that he wanted to address concerning the way in which teachers are prepared for the classroom (Duncan, 2009). One of these issues he stated was that "they [teachers] say they were not taught how to use data to improve instruction and boost student learning." This statement reveals an important problem that teachers are faced with in our current educational system. Although teachers and schools are inundated with standardized tests each year, a majority of teachers lack the skills and expertise to truly use test score data in ways that could be instrumental in improving student learning. Often, teachers lack the expertise and training to understand how they can use test data to assist them in the classrooms. It is very important that there are opportunities through teacher preparation programs and that through continued professional development exercises, teachers are able to get the training necessary, first to gain a deeper understanding of standardized testing and student achievement data and second, to gain the capacity to use that data in meaningful ways.

In response to this need for additional training and expertise, I suggest that educational policies at the national level should provide funding to state and local officials to provide technical assistance to, and foster professional development among, school teachers and administrators whose schools are struggling to increase student achievement. The topics addressed by the technical assistance and professional development activities should include the following:

- *Testing Special Populations* (including English Language Learners, Special Education, and underrepresented minorities): Research shows that the testing environment can be quite intimidating for particular groups of students. Teachers' awareness of the obstacles and circumstances that can hinder one's ability to perform well on standardized tests is essential. Ultimately, educating school personnel about these patterns will help students raise their test scores and provide them the opportunity to demonstrate their skills and abilities.

- *Understanding the Test Development Process*: In order to realize the purpose and utility of standardized tests, it is crucial that school personnel understand the test development process, particularly test design, development, administration, and use. Not only should school personnel understand the elements of the test development process, but they should also understand the manner in which these elements relate to one another and to the concepts of test reliability, validity, and fairness.

- *Understanding and Interpreting Test Results:* In order to utilize testing information to make progress, school personnel need to be provided detailed instructions for analyzing and interpreting test results. This will prove to be a useful tool in addressing the strengths and weaknesses of the school's academic programs and in evaluating the types of instruction best suited to improve student performance.

It is recommended that an educational policy be implemented and funding provided to struggling schools in order to assist them in meeting the objectives of the NCLB (2002), as well as to gain capacity in utilizing the resources that they currently have. Although we have the testing requirements in place, testing without the corresponding understanding among school personnel of the mechanics of test development and test interpretation is only minimally useful. Policies such as this at the national, state and local levels would help make the goals of NCLB much more feasible and useful.

High-Stakes Testing

Issues related to high-stakes testing have been addressed for several decades. In the 1990s several states began to implement standardized tests that were used for grade promotion and high school graduation. This trend has been extended to the twenty-first century, and with the implementation of NCLB (2002), has nearly skyrocketed. When I think of high-stakes testing, I am reminded of a student who was a senior at the high school where I was working. He was a talented and gregarious young man. He had managed to maintain a fairly good GPA and had received a scholarship from a college in the state. There was only one problem: After several attempts he could not pass the science portion of the Georgia high school graduation test. As a result, he was not able to graduate with his peers, and I never found out if he was able to pass the science portion of the graduation test during the summer and go on to college. Although this situation is somewhat extreme, it has often made me wonder, what is the cost of high-stakes testing to students? Particularly because there are differences in the way in which certain groups experience the testing environment, what are the ultimate costs?

What is the Cost?

To put a monetary figure on high-stakes testing, let's consider a high school graduation test. Research has shown that since the implementation of high school graduation tests, the drop out rate has increased. So we must answer the question, what is the cost to the student who does not pass the test and does not receive a high school diploma? The Alliance for Excellent Education, in a report titled "The High Cost of High School Dropouts" in the issue brief August 2009, conducted a study that compared the annual incomes of students who dropout of high school and those who graduate. The data showed that in 2005, a high school dropout made on average $17,299, while a high school graduate made $26,933. Over the course of one's lifetime, a high school graduate makes approximately $260,000 more than a high school dropout. Consequently, the research shows that the cost of not passing a high school graduation test is $260,000 per person. Multiply this amount by the number of high school dropouts each year, and one calculates a loss of billions of dollars in income over the course of a lifetime. For example, in the state of Louisiana, in 2009 approximately 20,011 students dropped out of school. The total loss in income over their lifetime is $5,202,860.00. This finding is especially problematic for particular groups such as Hispanic American and Black students, who research has shown to drop out of high school at a disproportionately higher rate than their White counterparts. By placing a monetary value on high school graduation tests, we can now understand why it is of utmost important to ensure that tests are fair for all groups of students and that the interpretation of the test scores are valid. As shown, the impact of graduation tests could be extremely costly to those students are groups who struggle with standardized tests.

Learning From the Past

Educational policymakers and government officials often review historical policies and documents in order to understand some of the issues and concerns that have been addressed as a result of earlier policies. The historical perspective helps one to craft new policy and legislation, while ensuring that some of the same problem areas that were present in other policies have been addressed in the current policy. In this same fashion, it is important that we examine historical events that are related to testing and issues of fairness. First, our current educational system relies heavily on the results of standardized testing. This substantial reliance on standardized testing is cause for concern. The concerns are not necessarily the issues or problems that are faced currently; the concern is about the consequences of these policies in years to come.

In an effort to address these concerns, we must ask ourselves what historical policies and events can help us to evaluate the potential effects of our current educational policy? Specifically, we must consider those policies, like the NCLB (2002) that use standardized tests as a means of accountability. As outlined in Chapter 2 on test fairness, during World War II the Army Alpha Beta Tests were administered to nearly 1.75 million Army recruits. Robert Yerkes, the Harvard psychologist who initiated the testing, claimed that the tests were measuring native intellectual ability and were unaffected by culture or educational opportunities. The test results were used in high-stakes decisions such as whether or not a soldier could enter officer training. The results not only showed there was a considerable difference between test performance of Black and White test takers, but it categorized European immigrants on their group scores as well.

Gould (1996) provides a detailed overview and evaluation of the Army Alpha Beta tests. In his critique Gould highlights the scientific racism that was exhibited on the interpretations of the scores of these tests. He then describes in detail why the Alpha Beta tests were not measures of innate ability, but measures of American society norms and one's environment. Although, the tests may have been administered to assess innate intelligence and were initially used to identify soldiers who were qualified for officer training, the unintended consequences and ways the findings were used outside of this were unfortunate and detrimental to many groups of test takers. First, the test results were used to defend racial segregation and were instrumental in limiting access of Blacks to higher education. Additionally, they were used politically in the debate concerning the restriction of immigrants coming into the country.

Some argued that southern and eastern Europeans should not be allowed to enter the United States because of their minimal scores on the army tests. In 1923 a scientist named Carl Brigham who worked with Robert Yerkes wrote a study titled American Intelligence (Brigham, 1923). His writings, based on the results of the army tests, were instrumental in restricting immigration of certain groups. Ironically, 6 years after his data had been used to implement immigration quotas, he realized the army alpha beta data were worthless as measures of innate intelligence. His realization was too late, it was estimated that the quotas kept up to 6 million southern, central and eastern Europeans between 1924 and World War II out of the United States (Chase, 1977). This is an illustration of how the unintended use of test scores can have a disastrous effect on particular groups and individuals.

Will future generations look back on this current time in history with the same disdain we have for the Army Alpha Beta tests? As I read information about the Army Alpha Beta tests from a contemporary point of view, I can easily see the problems with using them to make high-stakes decisions. For example, I can easily discern how issues such as time constraints, literacy, and anxiety could have an effect on the validity of the interpretation of the test scores. Did no one during that time understand the long-lasting cultural, social and psychological effects that using these tests in these ways would have on particular groups of people? One thing we have learned from the unintended uses of the Army Alpha Beta tests is that problems arise when we start highlighting the supposed intellectual inferiority and superiority of others and begin to sort and rank groups.

When we address consequences, particularly unintended consequences, we must visualize beyond where we are now. We must understand the impact these consequences will have on generations to come. What will future generations say about our current educational policies? What will be their criticisms? I am often worried about the way tests are used and how they will impact the livelihood of our children, not just academically, but socially, culturally and psychologically as well. As we compare groups and measure achievement, we tend to assume that the measuring stick is accurate. We decide that one group is inherently smarter or better than another. Many fail to address critical issues that may have an effect on these outcomes. This critical examination is important, as highlighted in the example of the Army Alpha Beta tests, because the consequences of such educational policies and the use of standardized tests could have dramatic effects on particular groups of students for years to come.

RESEARCHERS AND ACADEMICS

Areas of Further Research

The research that has been presented in this book examines issues related to the Black and White achievement gap. The research to date has focused primarily on these issues from multiple perspectives. Presented below are recommendations concerning areas that require further research. These areas have the potential to help address and provide solutions to issues related to understanding differences in test performance between Black and White test takers.

Fair is Fair

The information provided in Chapter 2 addresses the notion of test fairness. As discussed, there are multiple perspectives and interpretations of what test fairness is and what it should be. Of course, further dialogue and discussion should be focused on this issue. Given our current state of affairs concerning the focus on testing in educational policy, it is imperative that academics and researchers continue the conversation about fairness. They must help others understand the issues surrounding test fairness and propose ways to address fairness in all stages of the test development process. Most importantly, issues related to test use should be thoroughly researched and addressed.

It Makes a Big DIFference

Examining issues related to the Black and White test score gap has gone in several directions. Some of the studies presented earlier in this book have explored reasons or explanations concerning why certain items show DIF when comparing White and Black test takers. Research in the field of DIF shows great potential in helping us to better understand the Black/White achievement gap. Presented below are two areas related to DIF that additional research should be conducted.

Factors that contribute to DIF. The factors that contribute to DIF were discussed in Chapter 5. These factors were focused on a test taker's culture, interest, and the content related to the test item. This research has been helpful in understanding DIF on some test items, but it does not adequately address DIF on a majority of test items. Researchers have been trying to understand these differences more thoroughly. The research earlier in this book examines explanations of test performance differences related to test-taking strategies and the testing environment. The findings may be instrumental in recognizing reasons for DIF from other perspectives. The research in this area is very important. Additional research should be conducted that explores other reasons that can explain DIF between groups of test takers. Of particular interest is research that focuses on examining these differences from a cognitive perspective. As previously explained, these explanations can be beneficial in understanding test performance differences in total test scores.

DIF studies and standardized test gaps. Although many critics argue that DIF doesn't make much of a difference in total test performance, I disagree with their interpretation. DIF items that have been shown to favor one group of test takers in comparison to others are directly related to total test score patterns. For instance, research has shown that mathematics items categorized as measurement favor White test takers in comparison to matched Black test takers. In addition, the total test score information provided in Chapter 3 shows that on the NAEP, the mathematics items that were categorized as *Measurement* items had very large group differences between White and Black test-takers with the effect size as high as $d = 1.14$. In contrast, O'Neill and McPeek (1993) found that algebra items showed DIF between Black and White test takers. These items favored Black test takers in comparison to matched White test takers. The data from the NAEP tests show that algebra items had smaller group differences between Blacks and Whites in comparison to other subtests or content areas, with the effect size of the difference as low as $d = 0.86$. Consequently, we can make the conjecture that the larger the gaps between Whites and Blacks in total test scores, the more likely there could be DIF items that favor White test takers on that particular subtest. Similarly, the smaller the total test score differences between Whites and Blacks, the more likely there could be DIF items that favor Black test takers on these subtests. Based on these assumptions, we can estimate which types of items may or may not favor Black test takers on other tests. Research exploring the connections between DIF patterns and total test scores is important. It has great potential in helping to better understand the achievement gap.

Test Performance and Cognitive Processing

The research presented in Chapter 8 provides an examination of issues related to cognitive processing in the testing environment. Specifically, it considers how Black students process test items differently from White students in a high-stakes and low-stakes test environment. Research in this area is somewhat limited, so further research needs to examine the ways in which different groups of students process test items. This research holds great promise in understanding the impact that strategy choice has on total test performance. This type of research will require collaboration between those familiar with the standardized tests, such as education measurement specialists, and it will also require individuals with expertise in specific content areas, such as science, math, and reading. This type of collaboration will prove helpful in understanding the cognitive patterns of test takers and how they differ among examinees.

Think Aloud Studies

The research conducted in Chapter 7 in this book used think-aloud protocols to gain a better understanding of why certain test items showed DIF. Specifically, the think-aloud protocols were used to complement the quantitative findings based on the experiment that was conducted. Think-alouds could be extremely beneficial in understanding the causes of the differences in test performance on DIF items. Further, using think alouds in further studies that examine test performance differences will prove worthwhile. These types of studies can help us to understand the issues that students attend to in the testing environment and how they approach items and standardized tests in general.

Exploration of the Patterns of Similarity Between Black and Female Test Takers

Some of the patterns of differences between Black and White test takers are similar to patterns that are shown when comparing males and females. The test score and DIF patterns between Black and White test takers is presented in Chapters 3 and 5 in this book. Some of these same patterns of difference have been shown when comparing female and male test takers. On the NAEP, the test score patterns of differences between males and females show that on average, males outperform females in certain areas of mathematics, science, civics, and geography (Willingham & Cole, 1999). In terms of DIF items, there are a couple areas where the female/male comparison is similar to the Black/White comparisons. Specifically, females and Blacks perform better than their matched counterparts on algebra items and on items that include humanities content, human-relationships, or aesthetics content. However, males and Whites perform better than their matched counterparts on science test items, analogy items, and items that include a task that is related to the real-world and analogy problems (Gallagher et al., 1999; Hyde & Linn, 1988).

The similar patterns found between Black/White comparisons and male/female comparisons could be helpful in disentangling the reasons why these patterns of differences exist. To better understand these patterns the question must be raised, how are the cultural experiences and test taking experiences between Black and female test takers similar? The answer to this question is quite difficult to fully grasp. There seems to be a multitude of possibilities that can explain these similarities. First, one can argue that Blacks' and females' histories may provide the reasons for why we see these similarities. One perspective could be that both groups have dealt with issues related to civil liberties and oppression in the last century, such as the Civil Rights and Women's Rights Movements. Second, one could argue that there are similarities in relation to each group's cultural context. Based on research that was conducted in terms of culture, both females and minority groups in the United States are considered to have a high cultural context. Third, one could argue that the two groups' cognitive approaches to test items are similar. Specifically, Black test takers and females have been shown to use more conservative strategies on high-stakes tests (Arbuthnot, 2009; Gallagher & Delisi, 1994). These are all valid arguments that can be examined to explain the reasons why these groups perform similarly on particular items. This overlapping in test-taking experiences and performance between Blacks and female test-takers is a worthwhile area to conduct further research. Consequently, identifying what is common among these groups can lead to a more refined understanding of test performance patterns for both groups of test takers.

Hence, a greater understanding of these patterns will ultimately help to close the achievement gap in certain academic areas.

Using Research to Inform Policy

Most educational researchers and academics conduct research that is aimed to help inform educational policy. NCLB (2002) has called for such an increase in standardized testing, that it is imperative that we, the measurement community, be more proactive in providing more information to policymakers regarding the use of tests. For example, NCLB uses tests as a means to hold states and schools accountable for the education of all students. NCLB outlines a very ambitious educational policy that seems to use tests in ways that they were not necessarily intended to be used. As academics, specifically educational measurement specialists, it is our responsibility to share with policymakers and government officials our issues and interpretations of such policies. For instance, there is a wealth of information on how stereotype threat affects test performance for certain groups. This information would be helpful to policymakers and government officials when deciding upon how test score data can and should be used.

Integrating Research to Practice

As academics and researchers, it is often difficult to make the connections between research and practice. This has been an issue for academics over the years even in the way in which they write research. We must juggle the issues related to our own academic area and publishing in reputable research publications, but we also have a responsibility to practice as well. We must value research that addresses and develops innovative ways to integrate research and practice. Presented below are ways in which the research presented earlier in this book can potentially affect classroom practices. This is an illustration of the ways in which researchers can integrate their research findings to impact practitioners. For example, the NCLB (2002) increases the use of tests for most K-12 students. As such, this increase affects K-12 teachers in a multitude of ways. As previously stated earlier in this chapter, most teachers do not have the expertise or background to truly understand tests and test results in ways that could be instrumental in raising test scores. Issues such as this should be raised by academics and ultimately shared with policymakers. Hence, as an educational research community, it is vital that we all commit some of our time to service. This service would be to develop ways to facilitate greater communication and collaboration between researchers and practitioners.

Stereotype Threat and Test Performance

Arbuthnot (2009) showed that Black students performed better on certain items and processed items differently in the low-stereotype threat, or low-stakes condition in comparison to the high-stereotype threat, or high-stakes condition. The high-stereotype threat condition simulated a high-stakes standardized testing situation, while in the low-stereotype threat condition, students were told that the test items on the test were fair for all racial/ethnic groups of test takers. In an interview after taking the mathematics test, one student in the low-stereotype threat condition was asked about her experience while taking the standardized mathematics test:

> I'm like everybody got it right, I mean everybody got the same score, so it must be easy, so I did not get all nervous and stuff ... because on the tape it said that everybody did the same on the test, all the ethnicities did the same, and so I'm like well, obviously it's not like really difficult.

This quote illustrates the way in which the directions presented in the low-stereotype threat condition affected students in this group. As she stated when she found out that the test was fair to all racial/ethnic groups, some of the anxiety related to her taking the tests was relieved. She still had to take the standardized test, but just merely knowing that all racial/ethnic groups performed the same made her less anxious.

Although these findings show promise in understanding how race differences affects performance anxiety, it would be nearly impossible to implement an intervention that would tell students that the standardized test they were taking showed no differences between races. Equally so, it would be nearly impossible to control for the constant media coverage and other outlets that discuss racial differences in performance on standardized tests. That leaves us with a dilemma: How do we help Black students perform in a high-stakes testing situation in the same manner as they would in a low-stakes testing situation. There is no one answer; however, the overarching idea is that we must help Black students relieve the some of the nervousness associated with racial differences in test performance as well as help them to make the transition to perform as if they were in a low-stakes environment.

So, the answer is there are multiple perspectives and a host of ideas to help Black students make this adjustment. One way is to transition their thinking surrounding the high-stakes environment, ultimately trying to take away the pressure associated with this environment. This is not necessarily an easy thing to do. Further research should propose other interventions that may be useful in helping students make this transition.

Test-Wiseness

The research presented in Chapters 6 and 7, provided information about the ways in which Black students approached the testing environment. The findings show that there are some issues related to the test-wiseness differences between Blacks and Whites that can explain some of the differences in test performance. Specifically, the findings showed that Black students share in common the following test-taking characteristics:

- They have difficulty organizing their time in a high-stakes standardized testing situation.
- They use more conventional, or conservative strategy choices in the high-stakes test environment.
- They omit more test items than White students on rights-scored standardized tests.
- They do not finish as many test items at the end of the examination in comparison to White students.
- They persist longer on test items in comparison to White students.

The above findings based on research presented earlier in this book shows that there are some test-wiseness differences that can be beneficial to address with Black students concerning how to approach standardized tests. Based on these findings, I have devised ways that teachers and practitioners can use the information provided from this research to help Black students in the testing environment. In the next section, I provide a list of test-taking strategies that are aimed to address these issues.

TEACHERS

The research presented earlier in this book provides new information about issues related to the testing environment and Black students. The research findings provide the following four main ideas:

- Social and psychological factors contribute to the underperformance of some Black students on standardized tests.
- There are differences in the way Black students perform in high-stakes test environments in comparison to low-stakes test environments. Consequently, these differences can translate into lower test performance.

- There are differences between the ways in which Black and White test-takers approach particular test items.
- There are differences in the test-wiseness patterns between Black and White test takers.

As a practitioner I am sure it is quite interesting to read research that highlights new areas that help to explain the achievement gap between Black and White students. However, I am sure you are wondering, "Well, what can I do about this? How does this translate to practice? How can I use the findings from these studies to ultimately help my students?" The goal of this section is to integrate the research that I have conducted with best practice solutions in the classroom.

Quality of Instruction

The strategies and advice presented in this section are only complementary to high quality instruction. There is no substitute for high quality instruction in the classroom. Ultimately, in order for any student to perform well on standardized tests, he or she must have knowledge of the content and material being covered on the test. Therefore, the strategies and tactics are merely a complement to teachers' instruction of the content. For instance, if a math teacher focuses solely on test-taking strategies to help students excel on the math section of a standardized test, it will be moot if his or her students have not mastered the content that will be covered. There is no strategy that can substitute for understanding the skills in a particular content area. Consequently, knowing the material that will be covered on the test is naturally the first step in the process of preparing students for standardized testing. It is important to prepare them with the content knowledge, but in order to fully maximize their performance, you must prepare them to "show what they know" in the testing environment as well.

It's Just a Game

In order to help teachers better understand the ways in which they can help their students with standardized tests, I will begin with an analogy. I equate the idea of preparing for standardized tests to a sports team preparing for a game. Let's pretend you are preparing a basketball team for a game. Each player on the team has a certain level of skill and basketball ability. Some players dribble really well, some throw excellent free throws, others are good on defense, and some can shoot three-point shots with ease. Although the team has an enormous amount of basketball ability, they realize ability is not all they need to win in a game. In addition to each team member's ability, in order for the team to do well, they must have a strategy.

It is typically the coach's job to devise or develop a strategy for his or her team. Any good coach of a team has a strategy for his or her players to win games. How do you think a team would do if they had no coach and no strategy when they went into the game? They would most likely not play to their optimal ability, and consequently, the score would reflect this. It would be silly for a team to go into a game with no strategy against the opposing team. Although they may have great abilities, they may not be as successful as they would like to be during a particular game if they have not developed their strategy.

Prior to the actual game, a good coach will outline strategies to show his or her team how they should approach the game. How does a coach prepare his or her strategy? Most coaches prepare their strategy by doing research. They research the opposing team, the directions and penalties related to the game, and all other aspects of the game that could affect the team's performance. Based on the information the coach has collected, he or she devises the strategies for the game. The coach will then prepare the team based on the strategies that they developed. When a coach and a team have a strategy, they become more focused and have more confidence when they approach the game. In addition to the strategies on how to approach the game, a coach also provides psychological support to the team in order to build their confidence.

The above description of a basketball coach and team preparing for a game is analogous to a teacher and his or her students preparing to take a standardized test. First, each student in your class has some level of ability on different areas presented on the standardized tests. However, to maximize their ability, it is essential that the students have a strategy with which to approach the test. Consequently, the coach in the above example is the teacher. As the teacher, it is your job to lead the students and prepare them for the tests. This preparation involves two things: First, you, as the teacher, are responsible for gathering information about the standardized tests, as well as developing strategies that students can use while taking the tests. Once you have conducted the necessary research, you then decide how to prepare your students. You should show students what strategies or tactics can be used to maximize their scores. Additionally, you, the teacher, must encourage and prepare students psychologically as well. This will give them the confidence and assurance that they need to perform to the best of their ability.

I encourage teachers to explain this to their students. Help them to understand the roles of the teacher as the coach and each student as a player. Many may think this is too simple, but it works. The goal here is to remove the fear related to standardized tests. When a teacher describes the test as a game, students begin to see the situation from a different perspective. They will most likely be more engaged, and the idea that the testing situation is a game will reduce some of the stress and uncertainty related to the tests. The ultimate goal is to maximize the amount of points each of your team members make given his or her ability. In order to do this, a teacher must do two things. First, they have to prepare themselves and do the research. Second, they have to share what they learned and prepare their students. Presented in the remainder of the chapter are methods and strategies that will help teachers understand standardized tests and the testing environment for their students. The information can be instrumental in preparing teachers and students for standardized tests.

Teacher's Preparation for Standardized Tests

Although, the students are taking the actual tests, it is important for teachers to prepare for standardized tests as well. There are many things that a teacher can do to help their students do well. Presented below are several examples of ways teachers can prepare themselves to help their students with standardized tests.

Familiarity With the Examination

The first step is familiarizing yourself (as the teacher) with the examination. Take time to research the tests that your students are taking. It is important to understand as much as you can about the test. The more knowledgeable you are about the test, the more comfortable your students will be when taking standardized tests. Often, we underestimate how teachers' perceptions and understandings are translated to their students. As the teacher builds confidence concerning their understanding of the test, the student will, too. The following questions should be researched about the tests your students will be taking:

- What company develops the test?
- What are the test score distributions?
- Are there any practice tests available?
- Is there a database of questions in each content area?
- What are the directions for the test?
- How many questions are in each section?
- How much time do they have in each section?
- How was the test developed?

- Do your class lessons cover the material that will be on the test?
- What resources can they use on the test, such as a calculator, formula sheet, or dictionary?

These questions can easily be addressed by doing a little research. The research can be done online or with the resources and publications provided by the school. Next, if available, I would encourage all teachers to take a practice standardized test. The purpose is not to assess your ability or skills, but to help you understand the testing environment. By taking the test yourself, you can get a feel for the time constraints students will have, the way the questions are written and asked, and you can gain a better understanding of the format and directions.

Understanding the Testing Environment

To help students become comfortable and understand the standardized testing environment, it is important for teachers to understand the distinction between classroom and standardized tests. Why is understanding the distinctions between standardized tests and classroom tests important? Most students clearly understand the stakes involved in taking most standardized tests. Many students are told about the importance of taking standardized tests by their teachers, school administrators and their parents. Although students are told about the importance of these tests, they do not necessarily understand how to approach them. It is up to the teacher to assist the students in understanding how to approach a standardized test. The first step is to help them understand how standardized tests and classroom tests are different. For instance, it is not always advantageous for students to approach a standardized test in the same manner they would approach a classroom test. Although we assume that students understand the difference, it is important to highlight these differences to help them conceptualize and understand why they should approach these two types of tests in slightly different ways. There are 12 areas that I have found on which standardized tests and classroom tests differ. These categories include:

- Test directions
- Expectations of performance
- Performance effects
- Familiarity with the types of problems/questions presented
- The stakes involved with taking the test
- Time constraints
- Content covered on the test
- Teacher's control over the test

- Testing strategies
- Shortcuts and estimating
- Value of the test
- Use of the results from the test

As can be seen in the Table 9.1, the distinctions between standardized tests and classroom tests are significant. We make the assumption that students understand the differences and are able to attend to them appropriately in each of the testing environments. Understanding these differences helps students decide how to strategize on high-stakes standardized tests.

Table 9.1.   The 12 Areas on Which Standardized and Classroom Tests Differ

		Classroom Tests	*Standardized Tests*
1.	Directions	The directions for a classroom are typically familiar to most students. Their teacher explains the directions to the students prior to starting the test. The students feel somewhat comfortable with the directions because they are typically modeled after what has been done in the classroom.	The directions on a standardized test are not as familiar. Because most standardized tests are given yearly, the students have not had to deal with them in a while. The language used in the directions may be confusing and unfamiliar; often, a teacher cannot address students' questions as readily on standardized tests.
2.	Expectations	On classroom tests, most teachers expect that their students will do fairly well. Of course, there will be a distribution of scores; however, some teachers and students may expect to potentially answer all of the questions correctly. The assumption is that the information has been covered in class and the students should do fairly well.	On standardized tests, students are not expected to get a perfect score. The expectation is that students will miss some of the problems on the examination.
3.	Performance Effects	A student's performance on a classroom test typically only affects their score in the class.	A student's performance on a standardized test affects them, their class, their school, and their particular group affiliation (i.e., race, gender)

4.	Familiarity	On a classroom test, students are more familiar with the content being covered. They are fairly comfortable with the way in which the test is formatted, as well as, how the questions are worded.	On standardized tests, students are not as familiar with the content that is being covered. Specifically, they are not as familiar with the way in which the questions will be worded or presented.
5.	Stakes	Typically, each classroom test is only one score of many scores that will be used to calculate a student's grade. Therefore the stakes for each test are fairly low.	Most standardized tests are administered at least once a year and the stakes are high. The scores on the test impact students directly, their schools, their teachers, etc.
6.	Timing	Classroom tests may or may not have time constraints. Teachers typically give students ample time to answer all the questions that are covered on the examination. Time constraints are typically not as rigid in comparison to standardized tests.	Most standardized tests are timed. Consequently, it is important for test takers to organize their time well so that they have an opportunity to answer all of the questions on the standardized tests.
7.	Content	Classroom tests focuses on content that the teacher has explicitly covered in the class. The advantage is that the teacher prepares the test; therefore, he or she writes the questions in the manner that they were taught in the course. Additionally, students know specifically what will be covered on the test.	Although standardized tests focus on content that should have been covered in their classes students are not always sure specifically what will be covered on the test. They typically have more of a general idea about the content.
8.	Teacher's control	On classroom tests, the teacher has control over what will be covered, how the questions will be asked and the length of time that students are given to answer test questions. Teachers have the liberty to answer students' questions regarding the test.	On standardized tests, teachers have no control over the content that is covered, how the questions are asked, or the amount of time given to solve. Typically, teachers are not allowed to answer specific questions about the test while students are taking them.
9.	Strategies	On classroom tests, it is not as essential to use test-taking strategies when approaching test items.	On standardized tests, it is important that test taker have a strategy when approaching the test and test items.

Table continues on next page

Table 9.1.   Continued

	Classroom Tests	*Standardized Tests*
10. Shortcuts and Estimation	On classroom tests, particularly in the area of mathematics, students are usually required to show their work and are discouraged from estimating or approximating to solve problems.	On standardized tests, it works to the students' advantage to estimate and approximate on some of the test items. On the multiple choice test questions students do not have to show their work.
11. Value	On classroom tests, the correct answer and the method that students use to solve a problem is of value. On some problems students are given partial credit if they used the correct method but did not get the correct answer.	On standardized tests, the correct answer is valued. Specifically, on multiple choice items students do not receive partial credit. Consequently, the answer is of value, not necessarily the method students used to solve the problems.
12. Use	Classroom tests are one part of your grade for a particular class. Students are also given credit for homework, quizzes, class projects, etc.	Standardized tests are used for multiple purposes including: grade promotion, graduation, school funding, etc. The results of standardized tests typically effect other high-stakes decisions.

Preparing Students for Standardized Tests

Teachers should devote a small amount of class time to prepare students for a standardized test. This time should be focused not only on the content to be covered, but there approach to the test. We often leave kids out of the discussion when it comes to testing. We do not tell them the details about the test and what it is for and what it is not for. We leave them to their own interpretations, and that alone can send them into a whirlwind of anxiety. We emphasize they should do their best, but what does that mean? Presented below are several issues that can be addressed to help your students to succeed on standardized tests. The suggestions are based on research and personal experiences that have been shown to help students in the testing environment.

Understanding Students' Test Experiences

The first step in the process of preparing students for standardized tests is to understand the way students experience the test environment. Sometimes in our own naiveté, we forget who the real stakeholders are in this standardized testing game. We often feel that teachers, parents and policymakers are the important components to this equation. Actually, we must put the focus on the students. How do they feel about standardized tests? I believe this is a very important component of preparing students for standardized tests. It should be our goal to demystify the testing situation in an effort to maximize the performance of our students.

Utilizing Focus Groups. One method to better understand students' feelings and perceptions concerning standardized tests is to conduct a focus-group interview. A focus group is the process of collecting data through interviews with a group of people, typically four to six (Creswell, 2008). Although you may or may not have expertise in conducting these types of interviews, the steps presented below will give you an overview of the way to conduct one with your students. Please note that this is basically an informal approach to conducting a focus-group interview. If you are interested in conducting a more formal focus group interview, please read additional sources for a more detailed outline of the process.

STEP 1: State the purpose of the focus group interview

The first step in planning a focus-group interview is to decide upon the purpose of the interview. It is important to clearly outline the purpose of your focus group interview because it will help guide you through the additional steps in the process. For example, the purpose of the focus group interview may be to understand what factors concerning standardized tests make students anxious.

STEP 2: Identify the students who will participate in the focus group

The second step in this process is to identify the participants that you will include in the interview. This will depend on the purpose of your interview. For example, if the purpose of your focus group is to understand the way students approach standardized tests, you may decide to choose students who vary in their achievement levels. This would provide diversity in the type of information you receive. On the other hand, you may choose to conduct the focus group with high-achievers to better understand how you can help them to approach the standardized test situations. Therefore, there are several factors that you must address when choosing the participants, including (a) ability level, (b) racial/ethnic background, and (c) gender. You make the choice of whether you want the participants to be more homogenous or heterogenous.

STEP 3: Generate a list of open-ended questions that will be used to guide the focus group.

The third step in the process is to generate a list of questions. It is recommended that this list include mostly open-ended questions that give the participants the ability to elaborate on their feelings. The questions should be guided by the purpose of the interview. For example, if you are interested in learning about how anxious students were while taking standardized tests, it would be more beneficial to ask an open-ended question such as, "How do you feel when you are taking standardized tests?" in comparison to, "Do standardized tests make you anxious?" The first question allows the participant to open up and address all the issues that make them anxious in the test environment. However, the second question could potentially be answered by a simple yes or no.

STEP 4: Conduct the focus group

Next, you should conduct the focus group. During the focus group interview, you should steer the discussion with your questions; however, allow all the students to contribute information during the interview. By using open-ended questions, you allow the students to take the lead in the direction the discussion moves. Be prepared to allow students to elaborate on their feelings. Be sure to have some method of recording the information that you are collecting during the interview, such as a video/audio recording device or a note taker.

STEP 5: Review and analyze the results

Once you have collected the data, the next step is to review and analyze the information collected during the focus group. What did the students say about their experiences? Were there any common themes that many students addressed in the interview?

STEP 6: Use the findings to help prepare students for testing

The most important aspect of this process is for the teacher to gain a deeper understanding of how the students feel about testing and to help them alleviate any undue stress about the test environment. Lastly, use the findings to help tailor the ways in which you will prepare them for the test. For example, if the focus group interview revealed that your students express having difficulties with the time constraints on standardized tests, the teacher should share strategies and methods that will help them organize their time and pace themselves during the test.

Be sure that you address some of their concerns that were raised in the interview. Conducting these types of focus group interviews can help you understand your students' point of view, as well as help you to plan ways to reduce their anxiety and improve their strategies when taking standardized tests.

Low- and High-Stakes Testing Environment

With the increased focus that is put on the standardized tests, students' anxiety and concerns about taking standardized tests are increased. The research provided in Chapter 7 shows the ways in which Black students actually process particular test items differently in a high-stakes testing situation in comparison to low-stakes testing situations. Additionally, the findings show that students have more difficulty organizing their time in high-stakes situations in comparison to a low-stakes testing situations. These types of differences have been shown to depress test performance. These differences ultimately show that some Black students, when put in a high-stakes testing situation, receive scores that underestimate their actual ability level. Therefore, the question is, what can we do to help these students? One answer to this question is to help students perform as if they were in a low-stakes testing environment even while actually taking a high-stakes test. As can be seen in the first venn diagram in Figure 9.1, the high-stakes environment is seen as totally different from a low-stakes environment. However, the second venn diagram shows that the ideal testing situation is one in which Black students interpret and perform in the high-stakes environment as if it were a low-stakes environment. There is no easy way to ensure this will happen. As shown in Figure 9.1, the low-stakes environment cannot entirely overlap with the high-stakes testing environment. The basic notion is for teachers to help students adjust to the high-stakes environment as if they were in a low-stakes environment. Hence, the real question is, is it possible to do this? And if so, how do we help students perform as if they were in a low-stakes environment on standardized tests? One method, presented later in this chapter, is describing the standardized test as a game. This illustration is intended to help students feel like they are in a low-stakes testing environment when they are taking high-stakes tests. Further research should examine innovative ideas and ways to help students make this transition.

Knowing is Half the Battle

First, teachers must inform students of not only when and where the test will be, but also arm them with details about the test. The more information a person has, the less anxious he or she will be when Therefore, teachers should share with their students the information that they have gathered about the standardized tests. Convey to the students what you know about the test and what you have researched. A confident and informed teacher leads to a confident and informed student.

Figure 9.1.   Students performing as if they were in a low-stakes testing environment while actually taking a high-stakes test.

Test Components and Organization

Share with students what content will be covered on the test. This doesn't have to be an exhaustive review of each topic that will be on the test; however, let them know in advance what major sections will be covered on the standardized tests. This will reduce the anxiety related to the test's content being unknown. For example, an eighth grade algebra teacher preparing students for a standardized test, may tell students that questions related to factoring, monomials, and polynomials will be covered on the test. Additionally, he or she would remind students that these are all areas that they have covered and have been tested on in class. Making this clear to students will help them build confidence and potentially reduce the anxiety related to the exam.

Scoring

Students are often concerned with how they will be judged or evaluated on standardized tests. As a teacher it is important to relay to students how standardized test questions are scored and coded. The teacher must have an understanding of whether the test is norm-referenced or criterion-referenced. On norm-referenced tests, the students' performance is compared to the performance of other students. On the other hand, on criterion-referenced tests, students' performance is compared to a specified level of performance (Reynolds, Livingston, & Willson, 2006). Additionally, it is important to convey to students how each item is scored on the tests. Are the tests rights-scored, where a student either gets an item correct or incorrect, or is the test formula-scored, where students get a penalty for getting an item wrong. Last, the students need to understand how their final score is calculated. Teachers must explain to students the difference between a raw score and a scaled score, sometimes called standard score. Raw scores are the number of items a test taker gets correct on a test. Oftentimes, raw scores are sometimes difficult to interpret, so they are transformed into a different unit of measurement. Consequently, on norm-referenced tests, scores are typically reported as scaled scores, also called standard scores. The scaled scores are transformations of the raw scores to a desired scale with a predetermined mean and standard deviation (Reynolds, Livingston, & Willson, 2009). The information concerning the calculation of a score is important to explain to student's taking a standardized test. Students are very interested in how they will be evaluated and more importantly how their score is calculated.

"You Are Not Going to be Perfect"

In addition to discussing test content and scoring, it is important to emphasize to students that they are not expected to be perfect. Assure them that it is okay to miss some problems on the examination. Again, share with them how standardized tests are slightly different in this respect to classroom tests. Tell them that some of the test items may be a little confusing to them, and that is typical. However, the idea is that to answer questions that they know how to answer and try to answer them as best they can. This will alleviate for them the notion that they are expected to be perfect. Once they understand that it is normal for them to miss some of the problems or have some difficulties, this will help them to deal with the additional stress and anxiety they may experience as they feel pressured to answer each question correctly. For example, when they come across a question that is difficult for them to solve, they won't feel as guilty or lose confidence because they could not correctly solve the test item, because they are already aware that they are not expected to answer all the questions correctly.

Psychological Preparation

As discussed in the previous chapters of this book, there is a psychological component to taking standardized tests. Many students have some psychological impediments when it comes to standardized test taking. Research has shown that the test anxiety is increased in the standardized testing environment. Presented below are some ways that can help students relieve some of the anxiety related to the testing environment. These strategies are based on research and interviews with students and teachers.

Success stories "He did it, so can you." Sharing success stories of former students can have a profound effect on students' anxiety related to taking standardized tests. We are always talking about the deficiencies of particular groups of students or schools on standardized tests. For example, that Blacks overall do worse than others on standardized tests, and that particular types of schools are in danger of being closed based on their test scores, are both issues well publicized in the media. These constant triggers highlight a deficient way of thinking. Everyone wants to think that they can be successful. For example, when I taught a GRE preparation course to minority undergraduate students, I would always begin by telling them success stories of former students. When sharing these stories with my students, I would describe each of the test-takers in detail. For instance, I may say,

> Tonya, a Black student majoring in Sociology from California who attended Howard University, was in my course the previous year. She, was very anxious about taking the GRE. However, after taking the course and studying diligently she increased her score by 150 points in mathematics alone. Her final score for the mathematics section was 710.

Sharing others' stories of success allowed the students to make connections with the people I was describing. Consequently, they would hear stories of individuals who had similar characteristics to them, and this allowed them to think that they, too, could get a high score on the GRE. Needless to say, it worked. As I previously said, many students are inundated with the idea that they will not do well, or that their group traditionally doesn't perform well, and it creates a deficit type mentality, a feeling that their group will never perform well or be successful taking tests. As teachers you must change this type of thinking for your students. Help them to believe and expect that they can be successful on standardized tests.

Practice makes perfect. I encourage teachers to share with students practice problems and tests. Taking practice problems and tests helps to reduce the anxiety of taking standardized tests. Practicing allows students to become familiarized with the test content; however, it is equally important to practice being in the test environment. The more times a student has experienced this type of environment, the less likely one will be anxious. In addition, practice provides students the opportunity to practice test-taking strategies as well.

Test-Taking Strategies

Presented below are several test-taking strategies that I believe will help students increase their performance on standardized tests. The strategies are based on the research I've conducted on test-taking styles and differences.

"On Your Marks, Get Set, Go!"

This strategy is directly related to how one organizes his or her time while taking a standardized test. The research presented Chapter 6 discusses how test-speededness, or the rate at which one finishes taking a test, differs between Black and White test takers. Additionally, the research shows that Black students have issues with time organization when they are in a high-stakes testing situation. First, it is important for students, particularly on rights-scored tests, to focus on using time to their advantage. The research presented in Chapter 6 shows that Black students do not finish tests at the same rate as White students. Consequently, this is definitely a disadvantage for those students who could have correctly answered the items at the end of the test. For instance, the study conducted in Chapter 6 showed that Black students persist longer than White students on items that they are having difficulty on. This is problematic because it wastes time that students could be using on other test items, and at times, can have an effect on a student's confidence levels. Therefore, teachers should help their students understand the importance of managing their time effectively. Based on the directions given for a particular test, help the students prepare beforehand. Tell them the importance of pacing themselves and making sure they have ample time to finish the test items given the constraints of the test.

"Do Not Try Your Hardest"

The research presented in Chapter 6 shows that Black students tend to persist on items that they are having difficulties answering. Many parents', teachers', and administers' advice to students before taking a test is typically "Just try your hardest." This is actually *not* necessarily beneficial for students. For instance, if a student tries his or her hardest on every problem, he or she will waste time and confidence while taking the tests. With the time constraints that are attached to most standardized tests, this is not a good strategy. Therefore, I call my strategy "Do not try your hardest," which means that when you approach a problem on the test that you may not understand or recognize, and you do not know the answer, skip it or circle it and come back. It is much more advantageous for students to spend time answering the problems they do know in comparison to staying on one problem for long periods of time. Many times, I have found that students believe skipping test items is basically giving up on a test or conceding that they do not know how to do particular problems. As a teacher, it is important to emphasize to students this is not giving up on the test; it is actually being strategic.

"Taking Shortcuts is Not Cheating"

The research presented in Chapter 7 shows that Black students in a high-stakes testing environment tend to solve problems in a conservative, conventional manner. The study found that although they may know other ways to solve particular problems, that in a high-stakes environment they will not utilize other methods. Additionally, on classroom tests many teachers frown upon students taking shortcuts or estimating; however, on a high stakes standardized test, it is in some cases worthwhile for students to estimate or take shortcuts to solve problems. For example, in mathematics, on some examinations questions it could be advantageous to approximate instead of solving a problem completely. Another example is on a reading comprehension test; it is not always advantageous to read each passage word for word. Often, it is strategic to skim the passage and then answer the subsequent questions. Some students feel that skimming the reading passage on a test is cheating or taking a shortcut. Consequently, teachers should encourage students to take shortcuts when they feel confident that it will lead them to the correct answer. Overall, it is good to share with students that taking shortcuts sometimes can actually help them save time and potentially could be beneficial to their performance.

"That's What They're There For"

Teachers should encourage their students to use the options presented on multiple- choice test items. Generally, students begin solving problems without examining the options first. Using the options could actually help them eliminate answers that aren't plausible solutions or answers. Therefore, students should use their options wisely. Using their options in the test-taking process can save students valuable time and help them stay on track.

"Skip, Skip, Skip to My Lou"

When taking tests, students should develop a strategy to acknowledge when they should skip problems or simply guess. Specifically, on rights-scored tests, or tests that do not penalize for guessing, they should feel comfortable skipping items and guessing. Teachers should help students with a strategy for skipping and guessing. For example, if a student realizes after reading a problem that he or she doesn't immediately know how to solve it, the student should skip it and come back at the end. Particularly, in the beginning of a test, students should try to solve as many items as they can that are familiar to them. This helps to build their confidence and lower anxiety. Then, students often come back to items that they originally skipped and realize that they do know how to solve the item.

Additionally, teachers should be sure to help students develop a rubric for skipping items. One way to do this is circle the number of the skipped items in the test booklet. It is good practice for a student to put a random answer on the test answer sheet. This serves two purposes: First, it ensures that the student doesn't lose his or her place on the test, and second, if time doesn't permit them to go back to the item, at the very least they were able to guess.

CONCLUSION

This chapter has provided guidance and recommendations for several stakeholders, including policymakers and government officials, researchers, academics, and teachers. The purpose of the chapter was to show how research can be utilized by a host of stakeholders. The research can be used to (a) shape policy and help government officials decide on which policies to implement, (b) to produce new knowledge and information to stimulate new research, and (c) to help strengthen the teaching field.

First, this chapter has highlighted that it is the policymakers' and government officials' responsibility to address and challenge the appropriateness of particular educational policies. It is important that they are mindful and think critically about the unintended, although still relevant, consequences of current educational policies specifically, how these policies could have a disproportionate negative effect on certain groups. Second, the research and academic community has a great opportunity—and an equally great responsibility—to provide services to policymakers and practitioners. It is most important at this juncture in history that the research that is conducted in this area helps to inform both policy and practice directly about issues related to testing. It seems as if some sectors of the public believe that standardized testing is the magic tool that can tell us everything we need to know about a student. Of course, this is at odds with what we know as a community, which is that standardized tests are only *one* measurement that can be used to understand and identify a person's level of achievement. Even more importantly, research continues to address why certain groups perform differentially better than other groups on standardized tests. This research will continue to provide a refined understanding and interpretation of test score results. Therefore, it is imperative that the research community finds ways and mechanisms to share our work and insight with policymakers and practitioners. Last, it has been apparent that teachers and practitioners are struggling with the increased emphasis and implementation of standardized tests. Teachers are somewhat overwhelmed with the responsibility of helping their students succeed on standardized tests. Although quality instruction in each academic area is key, teachers should also utilize strategies to help their students excel and succeed on standardized tests. The strategies that were set forth in this chapter should provide a basic framework for teachers to follow in preparing their students for standardized tests.

In sum, it is vital that all stakeholders utilize research to help inform them on ways in which to craft useful educational policy, further the understanding of differences in the standardized testing experiences of different groups, and help students learn and perform well on standardized tests.

FINAL THOUGHTS

It has been a privilege for me to share my research, opinions and perspective concerning the differences in test performance between Black and White students. My intention for writing this book was to inform, inspire and at the very least, irritate. First, I hope to have informed readers about the information that I know that can have an impact on the way we understand and discuss the achievement gap. Second, I hope that something in this book has inspired you to take a closer look at our kids and the standardized tests that they are mandated to take each year. A deeper understanding about this process can help our kids learn and perform better. Last, for some, I may have irritated you with my theories and perspective on test performance differences. I am happy to know that some may criticize or reject my opinions and perspectives on these issues, but this type of disagreement encourages dialogue.

In writing this book, I took you through the research and work that I have been conducting for the last ten years of my life. This work has been at times arduous and frustrating because although I was learning and researching in these areas, I was always concerned with sharing the research in a way that it could impact student learning- namely test score performance. When I left Atlanta as a teacher to pursue a degree and conduct research, I had one goal in mind: make a difference. Specifically, I aimed to make a difference in the way people understand Black students' abilities, achievements and test taking experiences. What I hadn't expected was during my tenure as a graduate student and academic, the wave of standardized testing would grow so much stronger with the implementation of the No Child Left Behind Act (2002), making my work and research much more important, vital and timely. As I finish writing this book, it closes an important chapter and season in my life and career. It is the basis for what I have learned and the information I can share with the world about the Black-White achievement gap. It raises lots of questions concerning where we are now in our debate about test performance and the use of high-stakes testing in education. As this chapter in my life and career closes, I am in awe of what is ahead. I find myself asking, where do I go from here, with what I have learned thus far and with the information I feel like I know? That question lingers in the back of my mind. I will always be a teacher, from teaching high school to graduate school; that will never change. However, the way in which I use, disseminate and share my work and experiences in the field may change. I hope to one day accomplish the goal I set out to do as a young high school teacher, and that is to be a voice for the students who are frustrated and intimidated by standardized tests, especially and specifically those students who have awesome abilities which, for various reasons, aren't necessarily shown in their test scores. To conclude, I am overjoyed to have finished this project and am excited about the prospect of something within the pages of this book making a difference.

I will close with a set of letters I have written to stakeholders concerning standardized testing and the Black-White achievement gap. The purpose of these letters is to present a basic synopsis and overview of my own personal thoughts and perspectives concerning issues surrounding Black students and standardized tests.

Dear Policymakers & Government officials,

It is your task as policymakers to draft and construct legislation and policies that impact constituents at the local, state and national levels. When we talk about educational policy, the ultimate goal tends to be to ensure student learning. And we certainly cannot discuss educational policy without talking about the NCLB legislation. It is the first educational policy that has used standardized tests results in such a massive way. But this increase in the use of standardized tests has been the cause of great concern. The essence of the legislation is very admirable, as the intentions are essentially to provide an effective, quality education for all children. However, my major concerns stem from the unintended consequences that the policymakers did not necessarily expect or want to happen as a result of the legislation. We must address the unintended consequences and assess the extent to which they will affect our children academically, socially, culturally and psychologically. Although this is the first time in history that we have used standardized tests in K-12 systems at this magnitude, we can still look at our history to find small clues about the possible effects of such legislation.

For example, we can consider how the use of the Alpha Beta tests (See Chapter 2 for details) affected select groups of people. The results of those tests were disaggregated by groups, and people were able to sort groups based on their IQ scores. The assumption was that the interpretation of these test scores was basically valid. From a contemporary perspective, it is now fairly easy to see some of the issues with the test questions and how they were given. However, at that point in history, the Army Alpha Beta tests seemed to be a useful and adequate test. In this same spirit, we need to examine the uses of tests in our educational policy very thoroughly. The issue is not necessarily the current effects that we should be most interested in; it is the more lasting and unintended effects and consequences that we all must be concerned with addressing. It is my hope that the information provided in this book has been useful and informative in helping you to critique current educational policies and to be mindful of issues related to standardardized testing for future policies.

Sincerely,

Keena Arbuthnot
A Concerned Citizen

Dear Researchers and Academics,

Researchers and academics, especially those in the field of educational measurement, have a great opportunity and responsibility at this juncture in history. At no other time in history has there been such an increased interest in
testing. In the last decade, standardized test use has increased almost expo-
nentially. The requirements of the NCLB and increased accountability at
the state and local levels have contributed to this increase. Specifically, for
those of us whose research and educational backgrounds are focused on
educational measurement, it is particularly important to be involved in
assisting with the development and scrutiny of educational policy and the
application of our research to practice.

In this new educational landscape, we as educational measurement specialists must decide upon and define our role. What should this role be? As
many know the educational measurement and psychometrics field is a very
specialized field of study. The demand for this type of expertise is much
higher than the supply. Many are finding the job prospects outside of academia to be very alluring. Thus, the demand in the field should be an indication that there is an increased need and interest in the skills and expertise
that our community provides, particularly in the field of education. How do
we use this expertise to help both policymakers and practitioners make
sense of issues related to testing? These are issues such as how tests should
be used, issues of reliability and validity, issues concerning the limitations of
testing, and issues of fairness. These are all issues that can provide very
informative insight for a multitude of stakeholders. How can we facilitate a
more seamless affiliation and relationship with these stakeholder groups in
an effort to build our capacity to provide assistance and guidance in test-
related issues? In this book I have provided some advice and insight on
these issues. It is my hope that this dialogue concerning our role continues,
and that we take on a greater role in addressing issues of testing in educational policy and practice.

Sincerely,

Keena Arbuthnot
A Fellow Colleague

Dear Teachers,

As previously mentioned, I began my career as a high school mathematics teacher in Georgia. During that time Georgia had already implemented the Georgia High School Graduation Test. The juniors and seniors in the school were dealing with these tests, while some college bound students were also grappling with the SAT or ACT to secure their college entrance. During that time period, I had never been so inundated with the process and the pressures related to standardized tests. I am sure that each of you is dealing with standardized testing issues in your classrooms, as well.

Since the onset of the NCLB, nearly all K-12 teachers have to deal with issues related to standardized testing. Many teachers are dealing with the same issues you are. Most teachers want to ensure that their students are learning course material and can have the opportunity to "show what they know" on standardized tests. Many teachers are confronted with asking themselves, "How can I prepare myself and my students for standardized tests?" Particularly, those teachers who are teaching at schools with high minority populations, or schools that have in general performed poorly on standardized tests, are concerned about all of these issues.

In this book I propose several suggestions for teachers/practitioners in order to assist them in helping their students maximize their scores on standardized tests. In no way am I offering a magic wand that will expand the ability and successfulness of a particular group of students; I am simply setting forth some best practices and suggestions based on my research that aims to help teachers and students navigate the testing environment in a way that they feel comfortable and feel empowered to "show what they know." It is my sincere hope that the information presented to you in this book will help you and your students.

Sincerely,

Keena Arbuthnot
A Former High School Teacher

APPENDIXES

APPENDIXES BEGIN ON NEXT PAGE

Appendix A

Scaled Scores and Standard Deviations for the 2007 NAEP Mathematics

	Composite			Algebra			Data Analysis		
	Average Scaled Score	SD	d	Average Scaled Score	SD	d	Average Scaled Score	SD	d
4th Grade Students									
Black/African American	222	27	1.00	229	26	0.86	227	27	0.95
White/Caucasian	248	25	1.00	251	24	0.86	252	25	0.95
8th Grade Students									
Black/African American	260	33	0.97	265	33	0.86	262	38	0.92
White/Caucasian	291	33	0.97	294	33	0.86	296	37	0.92
12th Grade Students									
Black/African American	273	31	1.04	278	31	0.89	272	33	1.08
White/Caucasian	307	34	1.04	308	35	0.89	308	34	1.08

Appendix A Continued

Scaled Scores and Standard Deviations for the 2007 NAEP Mathematics

	Geometry			Measurement			Number Properties		
	Average Scaled Score	SD	d	Average Scaled Score	SD	d	Average Scaled Score	SD	D
4th Grade Students									
Black/African American	224	24	0.90	218	31	1.06	220	30	0.93
White/Caucasian	245	23	0.90	250	29	1.06	247	28	0.93
8th Grade Students									
Black/African American	257	32	0.92	250	44	0.93	258	34	0.94
White/Caucasian	286	31	0.92	290	43	0.93	289	33	0.94
12th Grade Students									
Black/African American	276	32	0.97	267	35	1.14	270	32	0.95
White/Caucasian	309	36	0.97	307	37	1.14	302	35	0.95

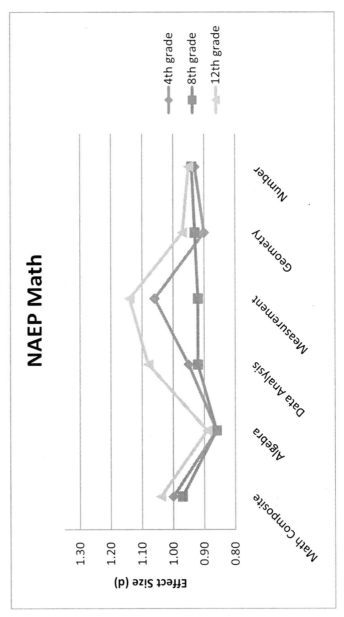

NAEP Math

Appendix B

Scaled Scores and Standard Deviations for the 2007 NAEP Reading

	Composite			Gain Information			Literary Experiences		
	Average Scaled Score	SD	d	Average Scaled Score	SD	d	Average Scaled Score	SD	d
4th Grade Students									
Black/African American	203	33	0.83	200	34	0.86	206	35	0.76
White/Caucasian	231	32	0.83	229	33	0.86	232	33	0.76
8th Grade Students									
Black/African American	245	33	0.85	247	35	0.76	244	36	0.79
White/Caucasian	272	31	0.85	273	33	0.76	271	33	0.79
12th Grade Students									
Black/African American	267	36	0.71	273	32	0.71	255	46	0.71
White/Caucasian	293	37	0.71	297	34	0.71	287	46	0.71

Appendix B Continued

Scaled Scores and Standard Deviations for the 2007 NAEP Reading

	Perform a Task		
	Average Scaled Score	*SD*	*d*
8th Grade Students			
Black/African American	242	39	0.80
White/Caucasian	272	36	0.80
12th Grade Students			
Black/African American	273	41	0.48
White/Caucasian	292	40	0.48

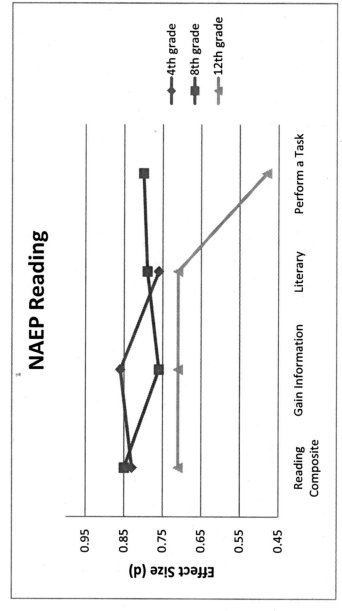

NAEP Reading

Appendix C

Scaled Scores and Standard Deviations for the 2005 NAEP Science

	Composite			Earth Science			Life Science		
	Average Scaled Score	SD	d	Average Scaled Score	SD	d	Average Scaled Score	SD	d
4th Grade Students									
Black/African American	129	29	1.19	129	32	1.11	128	31	1.08
White/Caucasian	162	26	1.19	163	29	1.11	160	27	1.08
8th Grade Students									
Black/African American	124	32	1.19	125	33	1.14	127	33	1.08
White/Caucasian	160	30	1.19	161	31	1.14	161	31	1.08
12th Grade Students									
Black/African American	120	30	1.20	117	31	1.21	123	32	1.06
White/Caucasian	156	30	1.20	154	31	1.21	156	31	1.06

Appendix C Continued

Scaled Scores and Standard Deviations for the 2005 NAEP Science

	Physical Science		
	Average Scaled Score	SD	d
4th Grade Students			
Black/African American	129	30	1.15
White/Caucasian	163	28	1.15
8th Grade Students			
Black/African American	118	35	1.20
White/Caucasian	159	33	1.20
12th Grade Students			
Black/African American	119	32	1.19
White/Caucasian	157	32	1.19

137

Appendix C

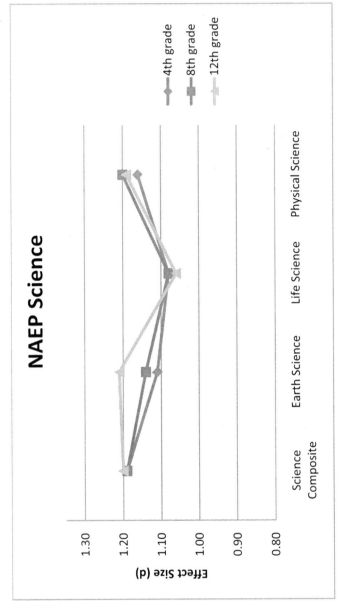

Appendix D

Scaled Scores and Standard Deviations for the 2006 NAEP U.S. History

	Composite			Cultures			Democracy		
	Average Scaled Score	SD	d	Average Scaled Score	SD	d	Average Scaled Score	SD	d
4th Grade Students									
Black/African American	191	32	1.05	176	42	1.02	203	30	0.85
White/Caucasian	223	29	1.05	216	36	1.02	228	28	0.85
8th Grade Students									
Black/African American	244	29	1.03	251	29	0.93	243	33	0.86
White/Caucasian	273	28	1.03	276	26	0.93	271	31	0.86
12th Grade Students									
Black/African American	270	28	0.95	274	23	0.87	271	36	0.80
White/Caucasian	297	28	0.95	294	22	0.87	301	38	0.80

Appendix D Continued

Scaled Scores and Standard Deviations for the 2006 NAEP U.S. History

	Technology			World Role		
	Average Scaled Score	SD	d	Average Scaled Score	SD	d
4th Grade Students						
Black/African American	193	32	1.09	204	25	0.97
White/Caucasian	226	28	1.09	228	24	0.97
8th Grade Students						
Black/African American	241	27	1.02	237	34	1.22
White/Caucasian	268	25	1.02	278	32	1.22
12th Grade Students						
Black/African American	270	25	1.01	266	31	1.03
White/Caucasian	295	25	1.01	299	32	1.03

NAEP United States History

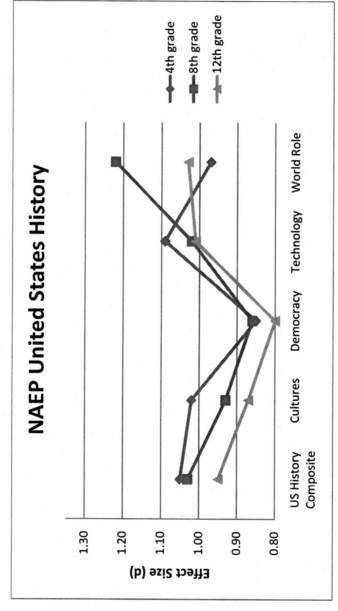

Appendix E

Scaled Scores and Standard Deviations for the 2002 NAEP Writing

	Composite		
	Average Scaled Score	*SD*	*d*
4th Grade Students			
Black/African American	140	33	0.62
White/Caucasian	161	35	0.62
8th Grade Students			
Black/African American	141	33	0.68
White/Caucasian	164	33	0.68
12th Grade Students			
Black/African American	137	31	0.69
White/Caucasian	159	34	0.69

Appendix F

Scaled Scores and Standard Deviations for the 2006 NAEP Civics

	Composite		
	Average Scaled Score	*SD*	*d*
4th Grade Students			
Black/African American	140	29	0.87
White/Caucasian	164	27	0.87
8th Grade Students			
Black/African American	133	34	0.89
White/Caucasian	161	30	0.89
12th Grade Students			
Black/African American	131	33	0.84
White/Caucasian	158	33	0.84

Appendix G

Scaled Scores and Standard Deviations for the 2006 NAEP Economics

	Composite			International			Market		
	Average Scaled Score	*SD*	*d*	*Average Scaled Score*	*SD*	*d*	*Average Scaled Score*	*SD*	*d*
12th Grade Students									
Black/African American	127	33	0.96	129	34	0.88	128	34	0.92
White/Caucasian	158	31	0.96	158	32	0.88	158	32	0.92

144

Appendix H

Scaled Scores and Standard Deviations for the 2000 NAEP Economics

| | National | | |
	Average Scaled Score	SD	d
12th Grade Students			
Black/African American	127	34	0.97
White/Caucasian	158	32	0.97

Appendix I

Scaled Scores and Standard Deviations for the 2001 NAEP Geography

	Composite			Environment & Society			Space & Place		
	Average Scaled Score	SD	d	Average Scaled Score	SD	d	Average Scaled Score	SD	d
4th Grade Students									
Black/African American	180	35	1.13	175	40	1.06	183	35	1.10
White/Caucasian	219	33	1.13	217	38	1.06	220	33	1.10
8th Grade Students									
Black/African American	233	33	1.16	235	34	1.17	231	34	1.21
White/Caucasian	269	30	1.16	273	31	1.17	270	31	1.21
12th Grade Students									
Black/African American	258	27	1.26	257	24	1.27	253	30	1.32
White/Caucasian	291	25	1.26	286	23	1.27	292	28	1.32

Appendix I Continued

Scaled Scores and Standard Deviations for the 2001 NAEP Geography

	Spatial Dynamics		
	Average Scaled Score	SD	d
4th Grade Students			
Black/African American	182	34	1.11
White/Caucasian	218	32	1.11
8th Grade Students			
Black/African American	234	33	0.98
White/Caucasian	265	30	0.98
12th Grade Students			
Black/African American	266	27	1.07
White/Caucasian	295	26	1.07

NAEP Geography

REFERENCES

Ackerman, T. A. (1992). A didactic explanation of item bias, item impact, and item validity from a multidimensional perspective. *Journal of Educational Measurement, 29,* 67-91.

Akiba, M., LeTendre, G. K., & Scribner, J. P. (2007). Teacher quality, opportunity gap and national achievement in 46 countries. *Educational Researcher, 37*(7), 369-387.

Alliance for Excellent Education (2009). *The high cost of high school dropouts: What the nation pays for inadequate high schools.* Washington, DC: Author.

Angoff, W. H. (1993). Perspectives on differential item functioning methodology. In P. W. Holland & H. Wainer (Eds.), *Differential item functioning* (pp. 3- 23). Princeton, NJ: Erlbaum.

Arbuthnot, K. N. (2009). The effects of stereotype threat on standardized mathematics test performance and cognitive processing. *Harvard Educational Review, 79*(3), 448-472.

Arbuthnot, K. N., & Ryan, K. E. (2005, April). *Black/White differences on a mathematics achievement test: An investigation of the content, cognitive complexity, and motivational patterns associated with items that show Differential Item Functioning favoring White test-takers.* Paper presented at the annual meeting of the American Education Research Association, Montreal, Canada.

Barton, P. E. (2003). *Parsing the Achievement Gap.* Princeton, NJ: Educational Testing Service.

Blascovich, J., Spencer, S. J., Quinn, D., & Steele, C. (2001). African- Americans and high blood pressure: The role of stereotype threat. *Psychological Science, 12,* 225–229.

Bond, L. (1987). The golden rule settlement: A minority perspective. *Educational Measurement: Issues and Practice, 6*(2), 19-20.

Brand, S., Felner, R, Shim, M., Seitsinger, A., & Dumas, T. (2003). Middle school improvement and reform: Development and validation of a school-level assessment of climate, cultural pluralism, and school safety. *Journal of Educational Psychology, 95*(3), 570-588.

Brigham, C. (1923). *A study of American intelligence*. Princeton, NJ: Princeton University Press.

Brooks-Gunn, J., Duncan, G. J., & Klebanov, P. (1996). Ethnic differences in children's intelligence test score: Role of economic deprivation, home environment, and maternal characteristics. *Child Development, 67*(2), 396-408.

Brooks-Gunn, J., & G. J. Duncan (Eds.). (1997). *The Consequences of Growing Up Poor*. New York: SAGE.

Brophy, J. E. (1983). Research on the self-fulfilling prophecy and teacher expectations. *Journal of Educational Psychology, 75*, 631-660.

Cain, G. G., & Watts, H. W. (1970). Problems in making policy inferences from the Coleman report. *American Sociological Review, 35*(2), 228-242.

Carlton, S. T., & Harris, A. M. (1992). *Characteristics associated with differential item functioning on the scholastic aptitude test: Gender and majority/minority group comparisons* (Research Report No. 92-64). Princeton, NJ: Educational Testing Service.

Carson, J. (1993). Army alpha, army brass, and the search for army intelligence. *Isis, 84*(2) 278-309.

Chase, A. (1977). The legacy of Malthus. New York, NY: A. Knopf.

Cohen, J. (1988). *Statistical power analysis for the behavioral sciences* (2nd ed.). Hillsdale, NJ: Erlbaum.

Cook, P. J., & Ludwig, J. (1998). The burden of "Acting White": Do Black adolescents disparage academic achievement. In C. Jencks & M. Phillips (Eds.), *The Black-White test score gap* (pp. 375-400). Washington, DC: Brookings.

Cole, N. S., & Zieky, M. J. (2001). The new faces of fairness. *Journal of Educational Measurement, 38*, 369-382.

Coleman, J., Campbell, E., Hobson, C., McPartland, J., Mood, A., Weinfeld, F. D., et al. (1966). Equality of educational opportunity. Washington, DC: Department of Health, Education and Welfare.

Creswell, J. W. (2008). *Educational Research* (3rd Ed.). Upper Saddle River, NJ: Pearson Education.

Darling-Hammond, L. (2000). New standards and old inequities: School reform and the education of African American students. *Journal of Negro Education, 69*, 263-287.

Dauber, S. L., Alexander, K. L., & Entwisle, D. R. (1996). Tracking and transitions through the middle grades: Channeling educational trajectories. *Sociology of Education, 69*, 290.

Dorans, N. J., & Holland, P. W. (1993). DIF detection and description: Mantel-haenszel and standardization. In P. W. Holland & H. Wainer (Eds.), *Differential item functioning* (pp. 3–23). Princeton, NJ: Erlbaum.

Dorans, N., & Kulick, E. (1986). Demonstrating the utility of the standardization approach to assessing unexpected differential item performance on the scholastic aptitude test. *Journal of Educational Measurement, 23*, 355-368.

Duncan, A. (2009, October). *Teacher education: Reforming the uncertain profession*. Speech presented at Columbia Teacher's College, New York, New York.

Educational Testing Service. (2002). *Preparing for the verbal and quantitative sections of the GRE general test.* Retrieved from http://www.gre .org/pracmats.html#gentest

Ericsson, K. A., & Simon, H. A. (1993). *A protocol analysis: Verbal reports as data* (2nd ed.). Cambridge, MA: MIT Press.

ETS Standards for Quality and Fairness. (2002). Princeton, NJ: Educational Testing Service.

Ferguson, R. (1998). Teachers' perceptions and expectations and the Black-White Test score gap. In C. Jencks & M. Phillips (Eds.), *The Black-White test score gap* (pp. 273- 317). Washington, DC: Brookings.

Flyvbjerg, B., Bruzelius N., & Rothengatter, W. (2003). *Megaprojects and risk: an anatomy of ambition*. Cambridge, England: Cambridge University Press.

Flyvbjerg, B., Holm, M. S., & Buhl, S. (2002). Understanding costs in public works projects: Error or lie? *Journal of the American Planning Association, 68*(3), 279-295.

Fordham, S., & Ogbu, J. (1986). Black student's school success: Coping with the "burden of 'acting White' ". *Urban Review, 18*, 176-206.

Freedle, R., & Kostin, I. (1997). Predicting black and white differential item functioning in verbal analogy performance. *Intelligence, 24*, 417-444.

Fryer, R. (2006). Acting White. *Education Next, 6*(1), 52-59.

Fryer, R., & Levitt, S. (2004). Understanding the Black White test score gap in the first two years of school. *The Review of Economics and Statistics, 86*(2), 447-464.

Gallagher, A. M., & De Lisi, R. (1994). Gender differences in scholastic aptitude test- Mathematics problem solving among high-ability students. *Journal of Educational Psychology, 86*, 204-211.

Gallagher, A. M., De Lisi, R., Holst, P., McGillicuddy-De Lisi, A., Morely, M., & Cahalan, C. (2000). Gender differences in advanced mathematical problem-solving. *Journal of Experimental Child Psychology, 75*, 165–188.

Gallagher, A., Morely, A, Levin, J., Garibaldi, A. M., Ibarra, R. A., Cohen, A. S., et al. (1999). *New directions in assessment for higher education: Fairness, access, multiculturalism, and Equity.* Princeton, NJ: Educational Testing Service.

Goodenow, C. (1993). Classroom belonging among early adolescent students: Relationships to motivation and achievement. *Journal of Early Adolescence, 13*, 21-43.

Gould, S. J. (1996). *Mismeasure of man.* New York, NY: W. W. Norton.

Graham, S. (1994). Motivation in African Americans. *Review of Educational Research, 64*, 55-117.

Gratz v. Bollinger, 539 US 244 (2003).

Hall, E.T. (1974). *Handbook for proxemic research.* Washington, DC: Society for the Anthropology of Visual Communication.

Hall, E. T. (1977). *Beyond culture* (2nd ed.). Garden City, NY: Anchor Books.

Hall, E. T. (1984). *The dance of life: The other dimension of time.* Garden City, NY: Anchor Books.

Hediger, M. L., Overpeck, M. D., Ruan, W. J., & Troendle (2002). Birthweight and gestational age: Effects on motor and social development. *Pediatric and Prenatal Epidemiology, 16*, 33-46.

Hembree, R. (1988). Correlates, causes, effects and treatment of test anxiety. *Review of Educational Research, 58*, 47-77.

Hernstein, R. J., & Murray, C. (1994). *The bell curve: Intelligence and class structure in American life.* New York: Free Press.

Hyde, J. S., & Linn M. C. (1988). Gender differences in verbal ability: A meta-analysis. *Psychological Bulletin, 104*, 53-69.

Jencks, C., & Phillips, M. (Eds.). (1998). *The black-white test score gap.* Washington, DC: Brookings.

Jensen, A. R. (1969). How much can we boost IQ and scholastic achievement? *Harvard Educational Review, 39*, 1-123.

Jussim, L. (1989). Teacher expectations: Self-fulfilling prophecies, perceptual biases, and accuracy. *Journal of Personality and Social Psychology, 57*, 469-480.

Kagan, D. M. (1990). How schools alienate students at risk: A model for examining proximal classroom variables. *Educational Psychologist, 25*, 105-125.

Kober, N. (2001). *It takes more than testing: Closing the achievement gap.* Washington DC: Center on Education Policy.

Kulick, E., & Hu, P. G. (1989). *Examining the relationship between differential item functioning and item difficulty* (Research Report No. 89-5). Princeton, NJ: Educational Testing Service.

Mayer, S. e. (1997). *what money can't buy: family Income and Children's Life Chances.* Boston, MA: Harvard University Press.

McDonald, R. P. (1999). *Test theory: A unified treatment.* Hillsdale, NJ: Erlbaum.

Meier, D., Kohn, A., Darling-Hammond, L., Sizer, T. R., & Wood, G. (2004). *Many children left behind.* Boston, MA: Beacon Press.

Messick, S. (1989). Validity. In R. L. Linn (Ed.), *Educational measurement* (3rd ed.). New York, NY: American Council on Education & Macmillan.

Meyers, A. F. , Sampson, A. E., Weitzman, M., Rogers, B. L., & Kayne, H (1989). School breakfast program and school performance. *The American Journal of Diseases of Children, 143*, 1237.

Millman, J., Bishop, C. H., & Ebel, B. (1965). An analysis of test-wiseness. *Educational and Psychological Measurement, 25*, 707-726.

Millsap, R. E., & Everson, H. T. (1993). Methodology review: Statistical approaches for assessing measurement bias. *Applied Psychological Measurement, 17*, 297-334.

National Center for Educational Statistics (2001). *The nation's report card: Mathematics 2000.* Retrieved from http://nces.ed.gov/pubsearch/ pubsinfo.asp?pubid=2006453

National Center for Educational Statistics (2002). *Digest of Education Statistics 2001.*

National Center for Educational Statistics (2005). *The nation's report card: Mathematics 2005.* Retrieved from http://nces.ed.gov/pubsearch/ pubsinfo.asp?pubid=2006453

Nisbett, R. E. (1998). Race, genetics, and IQ. In C. Jencks & M. Phillips (Eds.), *The Black-White test score gap* (pp. 86-102). Washington, DC: Brookings.

No Child Left Behind Act of 2001. (2002). Pub. L. No. 107th Cong., 110 cong. Rec. 1425. 115 Stat.

Oakes, J. (1995). *Keeping track: How schools structure inequality.* New Haven, CT: Yale University Press.

O'Neill, K. A., & McPeek, W. M. (1993). Item and test characteristics that are associated with differential item functioning. In P. W. Holland & H. Wainer (Eds.), *Differential item functioning* (pp. 255- 276). Princeton, NJ: Erlbaum.

Payne, B. D., Smith, J. E., & Payne, D. A. (1983). Sex and ethnic differences in relationships of test anxiety to performance in science examinations by fourth and eighth grade students: Implications for valid interpretations of achievement test scores. *Educational and Psychological Measurement, 43*, 267-270.

Phillips, M., Brooks-Gunn, J., Duncan, G. J., Klebanov, P., & Crane, J. (1998). Family background, parenting practices, and the Black-White test score gap. In C. Jencks & M. Phillips (Eds.), *The Black-White test score gap* (pp. 103-145). Washington, DC: Brookings.

Powers, D. E. (1993). Coaching for the SAT: A summary of the summaries and an update. *Educational Measurement: Issues and Practice, 12*, 24-30.

Rogers, J., Dorans, N. J., & Schmidt, A.P. (1986). *Assessing Unexpected Differential Item Performance of Black Candidates on SAT form 3GSA08 and TSWE form E43.* (Research Report No.86-22). Princeton, NJ: Educational Testing Service.

Reynolds, C. R., Livingston, R. B., & Willson, V. (2006). *Measurement and assessment in education*. Boston, MA: Pearson.

Ryan, A. M. (2001). *Explaining the Black-White test score gap: The role of test perception.* Human Performance, 14(1), 45-75.

Ryan, K. E. (1991). The performance of the Mantel-Haenszel procedure across samples and matching criteria. *Journal of Educational Measurement, 28*, 325-337.

Ryan, K. E., Arbuthnot, K., & Lin, C. (2002, April). *Investigating test item response processes for gender and ethnic groups on high stakes standards-based assessments.* Paper presented at the annual meeting of the American Evaluation Association, New Orleans, LA.

Ryan, K. E., Ryan, A. M., Arbuthnot, K., & Samuels, M. (2007). Student's motivation for standardized math exams. *Educational Researcher, 36*, 5-13.

Scheuneman, J. D., & Gerritz, K. (1990). Using differential item functioning procedures to explore sources of item difficulty and group performance characteristics. *Journal of Educational Measurement, 27*, 109-131.

Scheuneman, J. D., & Grima, A. (1997). Characteristics of quantitative word items associated with differential performance for female and Black examinees. *Applied Measurement, 10*, 299-319.

Schmitt, A. P., & Dorans, N. J. (1990). Differential item functioning for minority examinees on the SAT. *Journal of Educational Measurement, 27*, 67-81.

Sireci, S. G. (2004). The role of sensitivity review and differential item functioning analyses in reducing the achievement gap. In T. Kocher (Ed.), The achievement gap: Test bias and school structures? *Proceedings of the National Association of Test Directors.*

Spencer, M. B., Noll, E., Stoltzfus, J., & Harpalani, V. (2001). Identity and school adjustment: Revisiting the "acting White" assumption. *Educational Psychologist, 36(1)*, 21-30.

Spring, J. (1972). Psychologists and the war: The meaning of intelligence in the alpha and beta tests. *History of Education Quarterly, 12*(1), 3-15.

Standards for Educational and Psychological Testing. (1999). Washington, DC: American Educational Research Association, American Psychological Association, & National Council on Measurement in Education.

Steele, C. M. (1997). A threat in the air. *American Psychologist, 2*, 613–629.

Steele, C. M., & Aronson, J. (1995). Stereotype threat and the intellectual test performance of African Americans. *Journal of Personality and Social Psychology, 69*, 797–811.

Steele, C. M., Spencer, S. J., & Aronson, J. (2002). Contending with group image: The psychology of stereotype and social identity threat. *Advances in Experimental Social Psychology, 34*, 379–440.

Tatum, B. D. (1997). *Why are all the Black kids sitting together in the cafeteria?* New York, NY: Basic Books.

Vogt, P. W. (1999). *Dictionary of Statistics and Methodology*. Thousand Oaks, CA: SAGE.

Weiner, L. (2000). Research in the 90s: Implications for urban teacher preparation. *Review of Educational Research, 70*, 369-406.

Wenglinsky, H. (2004). Closing the racial achievement gap: The role of reforming instructional practices. *Education Policy Analysis Archives, 12*(64), 1-22.

Wells, C. B. (1985). Preschool literacy related activities and success in school. In Olson, M. P., Terrance, D. N., & Hildyard (Eds.), *Literacy, Language and Learning: The nature and consequences of literacy* (pp. 229-255). Cambridge, England: Cambridge University Press.

Willingham, W. W., & Cole, N. S. (1997). *Gender and Fair Assessment*. Mahwah, NJ: Erlbaum.

Zwick, R. (2002). *FairGame*. New York, NY: RoutledgeFalmer.

ABOUT THE AUTHOR

Keena Arbuthnot received a PhD in educational psychology from the University of Illinois at Urbana-Champaign, specializing in psychometrics/educational measurement, applied statistics, and program evaluation. She holds a master's of education degree in educational psychology from University of Illinois at Urbana-Champaign and a bachelor's of science degree in mathematics from the University of Central Missouri. She is currently an assistant professor at Louisiana State University in the Department of Educational Theory, Policy, and Practice. Prior to working at Louisiana State University, Dr. Arbuthnot held a dual appointment as a postdoctoral fellow and lecturer on education at Harvard University. Dr. Arbuthnot conducts research that addresses issues related to the Black-White achievement gap, differential item functioning, psychological factors related to standardized test performance, stereotype threat, test fairness, and mathematical achievement.

CPSIA information can be obtained at www.ICGtesting.com
Printed in the USA
LVOW08s0330190713

343643LV00005B/63/P